KATE HALE

Creative Arts and Cognitive

Growth Unlocking the Power of Imagination for Learning"

Contents

Introduction

C reative arts play a significant role in child development, serving as a key component in fostering cognitive growth. From the earliest stages of life, children interact with the world through creative expression, whether it's through drawing, painting, music, or imaginative play. These activities are not merely recreational; they stimulate the brain in ways that promote learning and cognitive development. Understanding the link between creativity and cognitive growth helps parents, educators, and policymakers recognize the importance of incorporating artistic experiences into children's lives.

The Role of Creative Arts in Child Development

Creative arts provide a unique platform for children to explore their thoughts, feelings, and understandings of the world around them. In the early years of life, children use art to express ideas they cannot yet articulate with language. Through drawing, for instance, children convey their emotions, perceptions of reality, and imaginative scenarios that help them make sense of the environment. This form of self-expression is a critical aspect of cognitive growth because it allows children to develop their understanding of abstract concepts and complex ideas.

Research shows that creative arts support the development of various cognitive skills, such as problem-solving, critical thinking, and spatial awareness. For example, when children engage in drawing or painting, they must think about how to represent an object or scene on paper, which requires the use of spatial reasoning. These types of activities challenge the brain to think in new ways, pushing the boundaries of traditional learning.

Furthermore, creative arts allow children to experience a wide range of sensory inputs. Engaging with different textures, colors, and materials enhances sensory processing skills, which are essential for cognitive development. The tactile experience of manipulating clay, for example, helps children understand the physical properties of materials, while also enhancing fine motor skills. These seemingly simple artistic experiences contribute to the development of a child's overall cognitive function.

Creative activities also foster imagination, which is a fundamental part of cognitive growth. Imagination allows children to explore possibilities beyond the constraints of their immediate reality, fostering creativity, flexibility in thinking, and innovation. Through imaginative play, children practice problem-solving, learn to adapt to new situations, and develop their emotional intelligence by role-playing different scenarios.

How Imagination Enhances Learning

Imagination is a powerful cognitive tool that goes hand in hand with creative expression. It allows children to create mental images, anticipate outcomes, and experiment with ideas, all of which are essential for learning. When children engage in imaginative play, they are not just entertaining themselves—they are developing critical cognitive skills that will serve them throughout life.

One of the most important ways that imagination enhances learning is through the development of abstract thinking. In many ways, imagination is the foundation of abstract thought because it allows individuals to conceive of things that do not exist in the physical world. This ability is crucial for learning complex subjects like mathematics and science, where abstract concepts must be understood and manipulated mentally. For example, when children play pretend, they are learning to think beyond the concrete and explore theoretical possibilities. This type of thinking lays the groundwork for more advanced cognitive tasks later in life.

Imagination also plays a crucial role in problem-solving. When children are encouraged to think creatively, they learn to approach challenges from multiple angles. Imaginative play often involves scenarios where children must solve problems or navigate obstacles, whether they are building a tower from blocks or navigating an imaginary adventure. In these moments, children are practicing the cognitive flexibility that will help them tackle real-world problems. They are learning to think outside the box, consider different possibilities, and try new solutions when their first attempts fail.

Moreover, imaginative activities enhance memory and retention. Engaging in creative arts helps children retain information by associating it with personal experiences and emotions. For example, when children create artwork that reflects something they have learned, such as drawing animals after a visit to the zoo, they are more likely to remember the details of that experience. This emotional connection to learning through creative expression strengthens memory pathways in the brain, making learning more meaningful and long-lasting.

Imagination also fosters a love of learning by making education more engaging. Traditional forms of learning often rely on rote memorization and repetition, which can be tedious and disengaging for children. However, when imagination is incorporated into the learning process, it becomes more dynamic and enjoyable. Creative projects, storytelling, and hands-on activities tap into a child's natural curiosity and desire to explore the world. When learning is enjoyable, children are more motivated to engage with new concepts and ideas, which enhances their overall cognitive development.

Furthermore, creative arts help children develop emotional intelligence by providing them with a safe space to explore and express their feelings. Art offers a nonverbal means of communication, which is particularly important for young children who may not yet have the language skills to express complex emotions. Through drawing, painting, or dramatic play, children can express their fears, anxieties, and joys in ways that promote emotional understanding and regulation. This emotional self-awareness is a key component of cognitive development, as it helps children navigate social interactions and build healthy relationships with others.

Additionally, imagination in learning promotes resilience and adaptability. When children are encouraged to use their imagination, they learn to cope with challenges and setbacks more effectively. In imaginative play, they may encounter problems or obstacles that require creative solutions. Whether it's figuring out how to construct a more stable tower of blocks or navigating a conflict in a role-playing scenario, children learn perseverance and adaptability. These skills are crucial for cognitive development, as they help children develop the mental agility needed to navigate the complexities of life.

Creative arts and imagination also foster social development, which is closely tied to cognitive growth. Collaborative creative activities, such as group art projects or dramatic play, teach children important social skills like communication, cooperation, and empathy. When children engage in artistic activities with others, they learn to share ideas, negotiate roles, and work towards common goals. This type of social interaction is essential for the development of higher-order cognitive functions, such as perspective-taking and moral reasoning.

Imagination and creativity also help children develop a sense of self and identity. Through creative expression, children explore their interests, values, and sense of individuality. Whether it's through creating a unique piece of artwork or inventing a story, children are able to express who they are and what they care about. This self-expression is crucial for cognitive growth, as it helps children develop a strong sense of self-confidence and self-efficacy, which are essential for lifelong learning and personal development.

Incorporating creative arts into the learning process is also beneficial for children with different learning styles. Not all children thrive in traditional, lecture-based educational settings. Some children are more kinesthetic or visual learners, and they need hands-on, creative experiences to fully engage with the material. By integrating creative arts into the curriculum, educators can reach a wider range of learners, helping each child develop their cognitive potential in a way that suits their individual needs.

The importance of creative arts in cognitive growth cannot be overstated. From fostering abstract thinking to enhancing problem-solving skills, imagination and creativity are essential components of a child's cognitive development. By encouraging children to engage in creative arts, whether through visual arts, music, dance, or drama, parents and educators can help them develop the critical cognitive skills they need to succeed in life.

Moreover, the benefits of creative arts extend beyond childhood. The cognitive flexibility, problem-solving abilities, and emotional intelligence that are fostered through creative arts are essential skills that serve individuals throughout their lives. Whether it's in personal relationships, academic pursuits, or professional careers, the ability to think creatively and use imagination to solve problems is a valuable asset.

Creative arts not only enhance cognitive growth but also cultivate a lifelong love of learning. When children are encouraged to explore their imagination and engage in creative activities, they develop a natural curiosity about the world and a desire to learn more. This intrinsic motivation to learn is one of the most powerful tools for cognitive development, as it drives children to seek out new knowledge and challenge themselves intellectually.

In conclusion, the connection between creativity and cognitive growth is profound. The role of creative arts in child development is not just about fostering artistic skills but about nurturing the cognitive abilities that are essential for learning and growth. Through imagination and creative expression, children develop critical thinking, problem-solving, and social skills that will serve them throughout their lives. By integrating creative arts into the learning process, we can unlock the full potential of children's cognitive development and set them on a path to lifelong success.

Understanding Cognitive Growth

Cognitive growth refers to the gradual and progressive development of an individual's mental capabilities over time. It encompasses a broad range of mental functions such as perception, memory, language, problem-solving, and reasoning. Understanding cognitive growth is crucial because it helps us appreciate how individuals, particularly children, learn and develop intellectually throughout different stages of their lives. Cognitive development isn't a linear process; rather, it's influenced by a combination of biological, environmental, and social factors. These aspects work together to shape the brain's ability to adapt and grow as individuals engage with their surroundings.

Cognitive growth is dynamic and multifaceted. From infancy, human beings begin the process of learning by interacting with their environment. Children explore the world around them through their senses, using sight, sound, touch, and taste to understand objects, people, and situations. As they grow, their brain becomes more adept at processing information, allowing them to learn new things, remember experiences, and solve problems more effectively. At the core of cognitive growth is the brain's plasticity—its ability to adapt and reorganize in response to new information or experiences. This plasticity is what enables individuals to continuously learn throughout life.

What Is Cognitive Growth?

Cognitive growth can be defined as the development and maturation of intellectual functions such as perception, reasoning, memory, and language. It involves the brain's ability to process information, solve problems, and make decisions. From early childhood through adolescence and into adulthood, cognitive growth enables individuals to acquire knowledge and skills that are essential for daily functioning and problem-solving.

At the heart of cognitive growth is the brain's plasticity, which refers to its ability to change and adapt in response to new experiences. This plasticity is especially pronounced in early childhood, when the brain is highly receptive to new stimuli and experiences. During this period, the brain forms new neural connections and strengthens existing ones, allowing children to learn quickly and develop their cognitive abilities.

Cognitive growth is a dynamic process that is influenced by a variety of factors, including genetics, environment, and social interactions. While the brain has an innate capacity for cognitive growth, external factors such as education, social interactions, and cultural experiences also play a significant role in shaping an individual's cognitive development. These external influences provide the stimulation and experiences that the brain needs to develop and refine its cognitive functions.

In early childhood, cognitive growth is characterized by the development of fundamental skills such as language acquisition, problem-solving, and memory. As children grow older, their cognitive abilities become more sophisticated, allowing them to engage in more complex thinking and reasoning. Adolescents and adults continue to experience cognitive growth as they encounter new challenges and experiences that require higher-level thinking and problem-solving skills.

Cognitive growth is not limited to childhood and adolescence. While the brain's plasticity decreases with age, adults continue to experience cognitive growth throughout their lives. Engaging in lifelong learning, staying mentally active, and challenging oneself with new experiences can promote cognitive growth and help maintain cognitive function in older adulthood.

Key Cognitive Development Theories

Several theories have been developed to explain how cognitive growth occurs, each providing valuable insights into the different stages and processes involved in cognitive development. Some of the most influential cognitive development theories include those proposed by Jean Piaget, Lev Vygotsky, and Jerome Bruner.

Jean Piaget's Theory of Cognitive Development

One of the most well-known theories of cognitive growth is Jean Piaget's theory of cognitive development. Piaget believed that cognitive development occurs in four distinct stages, each characterized by specific cognitive abilities and ways of thinking. His theory emphasizes that children actively construct their understanding of the world through experiences and interactions with their environment.

1. Sensorimotor Stage (Birth to 2 years):

During this stage, infants learn about the world through their senses and motor activities. They develop an understanding of object permanence, the idea that objects continue to exist even when they are not visible.

2. Preoperational Stage (2 to 7 years):

In this stage, children begin to develop language and symbolic thinking. They can engage in pretend play and use words or symbols to represent objects and ideas. However, their thinking is still egocentric, meaning they have difficulty understanding perspectives other than their own.

3. Concrete Operational Stage (7 to 11 years):

At this stage, children develop logical thinking and can perform mental operations on concrete objects. They understand concepts such as conservation, where the quantity of an object remains the same even if its appearance changes. However, their thinking is still limited to concrete situations and objects.

4. Formal Operational Stage (12 years and up):

In the final stage of cognitive development, individuals develop the ability to think abstractly and reason hypothetically. They can engage in logical thinking about abstract concepts, such as justice and morality, and can formulate and test hypotheses.

Piaget's theory highlights the importance of hands-on experiences and exploration in cognitive growth. He believed that children learn best through active engagement with their environment, rather than passive absorption of information.

Lev Vygotsky's Sociocultural Theory of Cognitive Development

Lev Vygotsky's sociocultural theory emphasizes the role of social interactions and cultural influences in cognitive development. According to Vygotsky, cognitive growth is not an isolated process that occurs within the individual; rather, it is shaped by social interactions with others, particularly more knowledgeable individuals such as parents, teachers, and peers.

Vygotsky introduced the concept of the zone of proximal development (ZPD) to describe the gap between what a child can do independently and what they can achieve with the guidance of a more knowledgeable individual. He believed that cognitive growth occurs when children are supported in completing tasks within their ZPD, allowing them to gradually develop new skills and knowledge.

Vygotsky also emphasized the importance of language in cognitive growth. He argued that language is a crucial tool for thought and that children use language to organize their thinking and solve problems. Through social interactions and communication, children learn to internalize the cultural tools and practices of their community, which in turn shapes their cognitive development.

Jerome Bruner's Theory of Instruction

Jerome Bruner's theory of instruction emphasizes the role of education and instruction in promoting cognitive growth. Bruner believed that cognitive growth occurs through the active construction of knowledge and that individuals learn best when they are actively engaged in the learning process.

Bruner introduced the concept of scaffolding, where a more knowledgeable individual provides support to help a learner achieve a task that they would not be able to complete independently. As the learner gains competence, the support is gradually reduced until they can perform the task on their own. This process of guided learning promotes cognitive growth by helping learners develop new skills and knowledge.

Bruner also emphasized the importance of discovery learning, where learners are encouraged to explore and discover new information on their own. He believed that learners are more likely to retain information and develop deeper understanding when they actively engage in the learning process rather than passively receiving information.

Bruner's theory highlights the importance of providing learners with opportunities for exploration, problem-solving, and discovery, which promote cognitive growth by encouraging active engagement with the material.

How the Brain Processes Creativity

Creativity is a complex cognitive process that involves the generation of new ideas, solutions, or products that are both novel and useful. While creativity is often associated with artistic endeavors, it is not limited to the arts. Creativity is essential for problem-solving, innovation, and adaptation in a wide range of fields, from science and technology to business and education.

The brain processes creativity through a network of regions that work together to generate and evaluate new ideas. While creativity involves many different cognitive functions, some of the key processes involved include divergent thinking, convergent thinking, and the ability to make connections between seemingly unrelated concepts.

Divergent Thinking and Creativity

Divergent thinking is a cognitive process that involves generating multiple possible solutions to a problem or multiple interpretations of a concept. It is often considered the hallmark of creativity because it allows individuals to think beyond conventional solutions and explore new possibilities. Divergent thinking is essential for activities such as brainstorming, where the goal is to come up with as many ideas as possible.

The brain regions involved in divergent thinking include the prefrontal cortex and the default mode network (DMN), which is a network of brain regions that is active during mind-wandering and creative thinking. The DMN allows individuals to make connections between unrelated ideas and explore different possibilities without being constrained by immediate goals or tasks.

Research has shown that highly creative individuals tend to have greater activity in the DMN, allowing them to engage in more flexible and original thinking. This ability to generate multiple ideas and explore different possibilities is a key aspect of creativity and cognitive growth.

Convergent Thinking and Creativity

While divergent thinking is essential for generating new ideas, convergent thinking is equally important for evaluating and refining those ideas. Convergent thinking involves narrowing down multiple possibilities to identify the best solution to a problem or the most effective way to express an idea. It requires logical reasoning, critical thinking, and the ability to assess the feasibility and usefulness of different ideas.

Convergent thinking relies on the executive control network (ECN), which is a network of brain regions involved in goal-directed thinking and decision-making. The ECN helps individuals evaluate the ideas generated during divergent thinking and determine which ones are most likely to be successful or valuable.

Creativity requires a balance between divergent and convergent thinking. While divergent thinking allows individuals to explore new possibilities, convergent thinking helps them refine and implement those possibilities in a way that is practical and effective. This balance is essential for cognitive growth, as it allows individuals to generate new ideas and solutions while also evaluating their feasibility and usefulness.

Making Connections Between Unrelated Concepts

One of the key processes involved in creativity is the ability to make connections between seemingly unrelated concepts. This process, known as associative thinking, allows individuals to draw on different areas of knowledge and experience to generate new ideas or solutions. Associative thinking is a hallmark of creative problem-solving because it enables individuals to see relationships between concepts that may not be immediately obvious. For example, an inventor may draw inspiration from nature to solve a technical engineering problem, or a writer might combine elements from different cultures to create a unique story. This ability to form connections between unrelated ideas is what often leads to innovation and novel solutions.

The brain processes associative thinking by activating multiple areas, including the hippocampus, which is involved in memory retrieval, and the temporal lobes, which play a role in processing and organizing information. When individuals engage in associative thinking, they draw on their past experiences and knowledge, searching for patterns and relationships between seemingly disconnected ideas.

One of the key factors that facilitate associative thinking is cognitive flexibility—the ability to shift between different modes of thinking or mental frameworks. Cognitive flexibility is essential for creativity because it allows individuals to break free from rigid patterns of thought and explore new possibilities. Research has shown that individuals who demonstrate high levels of creativity tend to have greater cognitive flexibility, which allows them to generate original ideas and adapt to new situations more effectively.

In addition to cognitive flexibility, working memory plays a crucial role in creativity by enabling individuals to hold multiple pieces of information in mind simultaneously. Working memory allows individuals to manipulate and combine different ideas, making it possible to explore new combinations and connections. The prefrontal cortex is heavily involved in working memory and executive functions, which are essential for controlling attention, planning, and decision-making during the creative process.

The Role of the Brain's Hemispheres in Creativity

The brain's two hemispheres—the left and right—play different but complementary roles in the creative process. While the left hemisphere is often associated with logical reasoning, language, and analytical thinking, the right hemisphere is more closely linked to spatial awareness, holistic thinking, and visual imagery. However, creativity requires the integration of both hemispheres, as creative thinking involves both the generation of new ideas (often linked to the right hemisphere) and the logical evaluation of those ideas (often linked to the left hemisphere).

For a long time, creativity was thought to be primarily a function of the right hemisphere, but recent research has shown that both hemispheres contribute to different aspects of the creative process. The left hemisphere's ability to process language and logic helps individuals refine their ideas and communicate them effectively, while the right hemisphere's ability to process spatial and visual information allows individuals to generate original ideas and think beyond conventional boundaries.

In highly creative individuals, there is often increased connectivity between the two hemispheres, which allows for greater integration of logical and imaginative thinking. This enhanced connectivity enables individuals to move seamlessly between divergent and convergent thinking, generating new ideas and then refining them into practical solutions.

The Role of Emotion in Creativity

Emotion plays a significant role in creativity, influencing both the generation of new ideas and the motivation to pursue creative activities. The brain's limbic system, which is involved in processing emotions, interacts with the prefrontal cortex and other regions involved in cognitive functions to shape the creative process. Positive emotions, such as excitement, curiosity, and joy, can enhance creativity by promoting open-mindedness and cognitive flexibility. When individuals experience positive emotions, they are more likely to take risks, explore new possibilities, and think outside the box.

Conversely, negative emotions, such as frustration or anxiety, can sometimes hinder creativity by causing individuals to focus too narrowly on problems or become fixated on rigid patterns of thinking. However, in some cases, negative emotions can also fuel creativity by motivating individuals to find solutions to challenging problems or express their emotions through artistic mediums. For example, many artists and writers have used their personal struggles or difficult emotions as inspiration for their creative work.

Emotion also influences the persistence and motivation needed to engage in the creative process. Creativity often requires individuals to invest significant time and effort into exploring new ideas, experimenting with different approaches, and refining their work. Positive emotions can sustain motivation and help individuals remain engaged in creative tasks, even when they encounter challenges or setbacks. On the other hand, negative emotions can either demotivate individuals or, in certain circumstances, drive them to seek creative solutions as a way of coping with difficult experiences.

The interplay between emotion and creativity highlights the importance of creating an environment that fosters emotional well-being and encourages creative expression. In educational settings, for example, providing a supportive and nurturing environment where students feel safe to take risks and explore their ideas can enhance their creativity and cognitive growth.

Creativity and the Role of the Default Mode Network (DMN)

One of the most critical discoveries in recent research on creativity is the role of the default mode network (DMN) in the brain. The DMN is a network of brain regions that are active when the mind is at rest or engaged in activities such as daydreaming, mind-wandering, or introspection. While these activities may seem unproductive, they are essential for creative thinking because they allow the brain to make connections between seemingly unrelated ideas and engage in divergent thinking.

The DMN includes areas such as the medial prefrontal cortex, the posterior cingulate cortex, and the precuneus. These regions are involved in self-referential thinking, autobiographical memory, and the generation of novel ideas. When individuals engage in creative tasks, the DMN works in tandem with the executive control network (ECN) to balance divergent and convergent thinking.

The DMN allows for the free flow of ideas and associations, while the ECN helps regulate and evaluate those ideas. This interaction between the DMN and ECN is what allows individuals to generate original ideas and then refine and implement them in a practical way. In essence, the DMN provides the creative spark, while the ECN ensures that the spark can be transformed into something useful or meaningful.

Interestingly, research has shown that highly creative individuals tend to have greater connectivity between the DMN and other brain networks, allowing for more efficient integration of divergent and convergent thinking. This enhanced connectivity may explain why creative individuals are able to generate novel ideas more readily and refine them into innovative solutions.

Creativity and Brain Plasticity

One of the most remarkable aspects of creativity is its ability to promote brain plasticity. Brain plasticity refers to the brain's capacity to reorganize and form new neural connections in response to learning and experience. Engaging in creative activities stimulates brain plasticity by challenging the brain to think in new ways and explore new possibilities.

Creative activities such as drawing, painting, music, and storytelling engage multiple brain regions and cognitive processes, including sensory perception, memory, problem-solving, and emotional regulation. These activities require individuals to integrate different types of information and think flexibly, which promotes the formation of new neural connections and strengthens existing ones.

Research has shown that engaging in creative activities can enhance cognitive abilities such as memory, attention, and problem-solving. For example, studies have found that individuals who regularly engage in musical training tend to have better working memory and executive function than those who do not. Similarly, individuals who engage in visual arts or storytelling tend to demonstrate enhanced spatial reasoning and language skills.

Moreover, creative activities can help protect against cognitive decline in older adulthood by promoting brain plasticity and maintaining cognitive function. Engaging in creative pursuits such as painting, writing, or playing a musical instrument can help older adults maintain cognitive flexibility, memory, and problem-solving abilities, reducing the risk of cognitive decline and improving overall brain health.

Creativity in Educational Settings

Understanding how the brain processes creativity has important implications for education. Traditional educational models often emphasize rote memorization and standardized testing, which may limit opportunities for creative expression and exploration. However, research on cognitive growth and creativity suggests that integrating creative arts into the curriculum can enhance students' cognitive development and foster a love of learning.

By incorporating activities such as visual arts, music, drama, and storytelling into the classroom, educators can promote divergent thinking, problem-solving, and cognitive flexibility. Creative activities provide students with opportunities to explore new ideas, make connections between different subjects, and express themselves in ways that go beyond traditional academic tasks.

Moreover, creative arts can enhance students' engagement and motivation by making learning more enjoyable and meaningful. When students are given the freedom to explore their creativity, they are more likely to be intrinsically motivated to learn and take ownership of their education. This intrinsic motivation is essential for cognitive growth, as it encourages students to seek out new challenges and persist in the face of difficulties.

In conclusion, understanding how the brain processes creativity provides valuable insights into the cognitive mechanisms that support learning, problem-solving, and innovation. Creativity is not just an artistic skill; it is a cognitive process that involves the generation and refinement of new ideas, the ability to make connections between unrelated concepts, and the flexibility to adapt to new situations. By fostering creativity in educational settings and encouraging individuals to engage in creative activities throughout life, we can promote cognitive growth, enhance problem-solving abilities, and unlock the full potential of human innovation.

The Science Behind Creativity and Brain Development

C reativity is one of the most complex and intriguing aspects of human cognition. It allows individuals to generate novel ideas, solve problems, and adapt to new situations. Over the past few decades, advances in neuroscience have provided valuable insights into how creativity emerges in the brain and how it contributes to cognitive development. Understanding the science behind creativity and its connection to brain development can help us better appreciate the importance of fostering creativity in educational settings and everyday life. The processes of imagination, the stimulation provided by artistic activities, and the impact of creative play on brain structure all contribute to cognitive growth and overall intellectual development.

Neuroscience of Imagination

Imagination is a fundamental component of creativity and cognitive development. It allows individuals to generate mental images, concepts, and scenarios that are not directly linked to their immediate sensory experiences. The brain's ability to imagine is rooted in a complex network of regions that work together to create and manipulate mental representations. One of the key networks involved in imagination is the default mode network (DMN), which plays a critical role in allowing the brain to think beyond the present moment and explore hypothetical scenarios.

The DMN consists of several brain regions, including the medial prefrontal cortex, the posterior cingulate cortex, and the precuneus. These regions are typically active when individuals are not focused on external tasks, such as during daydreaming, mind-wandering, or reflecting on personal experiences. Imagination often occurs during periods of rest or relaxation, when the brain is free to explore new ideas without the constraints of immediate goals or tasks. This ability to engage in mental simulations is essential for problem-solving, innovation, and creative thinking.

One of the most fascinating aspects of the neuroscience of imagination is its connection to episodic memory, which allows individuals to recall past experiences and use them to generate new ideas or scenarios. The hippocampus, a region of the brain involved in memory formation, plays a crucial role in supporting imagination by retrieving memories and using them to construct novel mental representations. When individuals imagine future events or hypothetical situations, they often draw on their past experiences to inform their mental simulations.

In addition to the DMN and hippocampus, the prefrontal cortex is another critical region involved in imagination. The prefrontal cortex is responsible for higher-order cognitive functions such as planning, decision-making, and executive control. During imaginative thinking, the prefrontal cortex helps individuals organize and structure their ideas, allowing them to generate coherent mental images and explore different possibilities. This process is particularly important for divergent thinking, which involves generating multiple possible solutions to a problem or multiple interpretations of a concept.

Divergent thinking is often considered the hallmark of creativity because it allows individuals to think beyond conventional solutions and explore new possibilities. Neuroscientific research has shown that individuals who engage in imaginative thinking tend to have greater activation in the prefrontal cortex and other regions associated with cognitive flexibility and problem-solving.

This suggests that imagination is not just a passive process of daydreaming but an active and dynamic cognitive function that supports creativity and innovation.

Another important aspect of the neuroscience of imagination is its role in theory of mind, which refers to the ability to understand and predict the thoughts, beliefs, and intentions of others. When individuals engage in imaginative thinking, they often simulate the perspectives of other people, allowing them to better understand social interactions and navigate complex social situations. This ability to imagine the mental states of others is essential for empathy, cooperation, and effective communication.

The neuroscience of imagination highlights the importance of fostering imaginative thinking in educational settings and everyday life. By encouraging individuals to engage in creative activities that promote imagination, such as storytelling, role-playing, and artistic expression, we can enhance their cognitive flexibility, problem-solving abilities, and social understanding. Imagination is not just a form of escapism; it is a powerful cognitive tool that supports intellectual development and innovation.

How Art Stimulates Cognitive Functioning

Art is one of the most effective ways to stimulate cognitive functioning and promote brain development. Engaging in artistic activities such as drawing, painting, sculpting, and music-making involves a wide range of cognitive processes, including sensory perception, motor coordination, memory, and emotional regulation. Neuroscientific research has shown that artistic expression activates multiple brain regions, enhancing cognitive flexibility, problem-solving, and overall intellectual growth.

One of the key ways that art stimulates cognitive functioning is by engaging the brain's visual processing system. When individuals engage in visual arts such as drawing or painting, they must carefully observe their environment, pay attention to details, and translate what they see into a visual representation. This process involves the activation of the occipital lobes, which are responsible for processing visual information, as well as the parietal lobes, which help integrate visual information with spatial awareness and motor control.

In addition to enhancing visual perception, engaging in art also stimulates fine motor skills and hand-eye coordination. The cerebellum, a region of the brain involved in motor control, plays a key role in coordinating the precise movements required for artistic activities such as drawing or sculpting. By practicing these fine motor skills, individuals can improve their dexterity, coordination, and spatial awareness, all of which contribute to cognitive growth.

Art also promotes memory and attention by requiring individuals to focus on details, remember visual patterns, and recall previous experiences. For example, when creating a piece of artwork, individuals often draw on their memories of past experiences, images, or emotions to inform their artistic decisions. This process of recalling and integrating memories activates the hippocampus and other memory-related brain regions, strengthening the neural connections involved in memory formation and retrieval.

Moreover, art stimulates emotional processing and empathy by providing individuals with a means of expressing their feelings and understanding the emotions of others. The limbic system, which is involved in emotional regulation, interacts with brain regions responsible for creativity and artistic expression, allowing individuals to convey their emotions through visual or auditory mediums. This process not only enhances emotional intelligence but also helps individuals develop a deeper understanding of their own emotions and the emotions of others.

One of the most significant ways that art stimulates cognitive functioning is by promoting problem-solving and critical thinking. Creating a piece of art often involves overcoming challenges, making decisions, and experimenting with different techniques or materials. For example, an artist may need to solve technical problems related to composition, color theory, or perspective, requiring them to think critically and explore different solutions. This process of trial and error stimulates the prefrontal cortex, which is responsible for higher-order cognitive functions such as decision-making, planning, and problem-solving.

Art also encourages creativity by allowing individuals to explore new ideas, make connections between unrelated concepts, and express themselves in unique ways. Engaging in artistic activities promotes divergent thinking, which is essential for generating original ideas and solutions. Neuroscientific research has shown that individuals who engage in creative arts tend to have greater activation in brain regions associated with cognitive flexibility, such as the prefrontal cortex and anterior cingulate cortex. These regions help individuals shift between different modes of thinking, explore new possibilities, and make creative decisions.

The cognitive benefits of art are not limited to childhood; adults who engage in artistic activities also experience enhanced cognitive functioning and brain health. Research has shown that older adults who regularly engage in creative arts such as painting, music, or writing tend to have better memory, attention, and cognitive flexibility than those who do not. Engaging in artistic activities can also help protect against cognitive decline in older adulthood by promoting brain plasticity and maintaining neural connections.

In educational settings, incorporating art into the curriculum can enhance students' cognitive development and academic performance. Studies have shown that students who participate in arts education tend to perform better in subjects such as mathematics, reading, and science. This is because the cognitive skills developed through artistic expression, such as problem-solving, critical thinking, and attention to detail, transfer to other academic domains. By fostering creativity and cognitive flexibility through art, educators can help students develop the intellectual tools they need to succeed in school and beyond.

Creative Play and Its Impact on Brain Structure

Creative play is a critical component of cognitive development, particularly during early childhood. Through imaginative and exploratory activities, children develop essential cognitive, social, and emotional skills that lay the foundation for lifelong learning. Neuroscientific research has shown that creative play has a profound impact on brain structure, promoting brain plasticity, enhancing neural connections, and supporting the development of higher-order cognitive functions.

One of the key ways that creative play impacts brain structure is by promoting synaptogenesis, the process by which new synapses (connections between neurons) are formed. During early childhood, the brain undergoes rapid synaptogenesis, particularly in regions involved in sensory processing, motor control, and executive functions. Creative play provides the stimulation and experiences that drive this process, allowing the brain to form and strengthen the neural connections that support cognitive growth.

For example, when children engage in pretend play or role-playing, they are not only using their imagination but also practicing important cognitive functions such as problem-solving, perspective-taking, and social reasoning. These activities activate brain regions such as the prefrontal cortex (involved in decision-making and planning) and the temporal lobes (involved in language and memory), promoting the development of higher-order cognitive functions. By engaging in imaginative scenarios, children practice the cognitive skills that will later be used for more complex tasks such as academic learning and social interactions.

Creative play also supports the development of executive functions, which are the cognitive processes that allow individuals to control their thoughts, emotions, and actions. Executive functions include skills such as working memory, cognitive flexibility, and inhibitory control, all of which are essential for goal-directed behavior and problem-solving. When children engage in creative play, they practice these skills by navigating imaginative scenarios that require planning, decision-making, and adapting to new situations. For example, during pretend play, a child might take on the role of a doctor, which requires them to remember various steps in treating a patient, think flexibly to adapt their actions based on the "patient's" needs, and control their impulses to stay in character. These types of play activities promote the development of the prefrontal cortex, which is responsible for executive functions and self-regulation.

The importance of creative play in brain development extends beyond the immediate benefits of synaptogenesis and executive function development. Research has shown that creative play also enhances cognitive flexibility, which is the ability to switch between different mental tasks or perspectives. Cognitive flexibility is essential for problem-solving, as it allows individuals to approach challenges from multiple angles and explore various solutions. When children engage in creative play, they practice cognitive flexibility by imagining different scenarios, shifting between roles, and adapting their behavior based on the evolving dynamics of the play.

For example, in a game of "make-believe," a child might switch between playing the role of a hero and a villain, exploring different perspectives and outcomes. This ability to shift between different mental frameworks helps children develop the mental agility needed to solve problems and think creatively. Neuroscientific studies have shown that children who engage in creative play tend to have greater activation in brain regions associated with cognitive flexibility, such as the anterior cingulate cortex and the dorsolateral prefrontal cortex. These regions help individuals regulate their thoughts, manage conflicting information, and adapt to changing environments, all of which are essential for cognitive growth.

Creative play also has a profound impact on language development and communication skills. When children engage in imaginative play, they often use language to negotiate roles, express their ideas, and communicate with their playmates. This type of language use promotes the development of the left hemisphere of the brain, particularly regions such as Broca's area and Wernicke's area, which are involved in speech production and comprehension. By practicing language skills during play, children develop their vocabulary, sentence structure, and conversational abilities, all of which contribute to cognitive development.

In addition to promoting language development, creative play helps children develop social cognition and empathy. When children engage in role-playing or pretend play, they often take on the perspectives of others, imagining how different characters or people might think or feel. This ability to understand and simulate the mental states of others is known as theory of mind, which is a critical aspect of social cognition. By practicing theory of mind during play, children develop empathy and improve their ability to navigate social interactions.

For example, a child pretending to be a teacher might think about how their "students" are feeling and what they need to learn, helping the child develop perspective-taking skills. This type of social understanding is essential for cognitive growth because it allows children to build relationships, collaborate with others, and understand the nuances of social interactions. Neuroscientific research has shown that creative play activates brain regions involved in social cognition, such as the medial prefrontal cortex and the temporoparietal junction, which help individuals understand and predict the thoughts and actions of others.

Creative play also promotes emotional regulation by providing children with a safe space to explore and express their emotions. During play, children can act out different emotional scenarios, practice coping strategies, and experiment with different ways of managing their feelings. This process helps children develop emotional intelligence and self-regulation, which are essential for cognitive growth. By practicing emotional regulation during play, children learn to manage their impulses, handle frustration, and navigate complex emotional situations.

The limbic system, which is responsible for processing emotions, interacts with brain regions involved in executive functions and cognitive control, allowing children to integrate their emotions with their decision-making processes. For example, a child who becomes frustrated during a game might learn to take deep breaths and try again, developing the emotional regulation skills needed to persist in challenging tasks. This type of emotional resilience is critical for cognitive development because it allows children to stay engaged with learning and problem-solving, even when they encounter difficulties.

Creative play is not only beneficial for cognitive and emotional development in childhood but also lays the foundation for lifelong creativity and innovation. By fostering imagination, problem-solving, and cognitive flexibility, creative play helps individuals develop the intellectual tools they need to succeed in various domains, from academics to professional careers. Neuroscientific research has shown that individuals who engage in creative activities throughout their lives tend to have better cognitive function, greater brain plasticity, and enhanced problem-solving abilities.

One of the most significant long-term benefits of creative play is its role in promoting brain plasticity, which refers to the brain's ability to reorganize and form new neural connections in response to learning and experience. Brain plasticity is most pronounced during childhood, but it continues throughout life, particularly in individuals who engage in creative and intellectually stimulating activities. Creative play helps build the neural foundations for lifelong learning by promoting the formation of new synapses and strengthening existing ones.

Moreover, creative play can help protect against cognitive decline in older adulthood. Engaging in creative activities such as painting, writing, or playing music has been shown to enhance cognitive function and reduce the risk of neurodegenerative diseases such as Alzheimer's. By promoting brain plasticity and cognitive flexibility, creative play helps individuals maintain their intellectual abilities as they age, allowing them to stay mentally sharp and engaged in life.

In educational settings, fostering creative play is essential for promoting cognitive growth and academic success. Research has shown that children who engage in creative play tend to perform better in school, particularly in subjects such as mathematics, reading, and science. This is because the cognitive skills developed through play, such as problem-solving, critical thinking, and cognitive flexibility, transfer to other academic domains. By incorporating creative play into the curriculum, educators can help students develop the intellectual tools they need to succeed in school and beyond.

In conclusion, creative play has a profound impact on brain structure and cognitive development. By promoting synaptogenesis, enhancing cognitive flexibility, and supporting the development of executive functions, creative play helps children develop the intellectual, social, and emotional skills they need to thrive. The neuroscience of creative play highlights the importance of providing children with opportunities for imaginative and exploratory activities, both in educational settings and at home. By fostering creativity through play, we can help children unlock their full cognitive potential and set them on a path to lifelong learning and success.

The Role of Visual Arts in Cognitive Development

T he visual arts, which include drawing, painting, and sculpting, play an instrumental role in cognitive development, especially during childhood but continuing through adulthood. Engaging in these artistic activities stimulates a variety of mental processes that are crucial for developing thinking, memory, and spatial awareness. Moreover, the physical act of creating art requires the use of fine motor skills, which in turn support broader cognitive growth. By understanding how visual arts contribute to cognitive development, we can appreciate the importance of integrating these activities into both educational and personal development contexts.

How Drawing, Painting, and Sculpting Stimulate Thought Processes

Drawing, painting, and sculpting are not merely artistic expressions; they are complex cognitive activities that involve critical thinking, problem-solving, and the organization of ideas. These activities engage multiple brain regions, requiring individuals to process information, make decisions, and execute precise actions, all of which contribute to overall cognitive development.

Drawing involves the transformation of abstract thoughts into visual forms, requiring the brain to translate concepts into lines, shapes, and textures. When an individual draws, they are engaging in a process of decision-making: what to include, how to represent different aspects of their subject, and how

29

to organize the composition on the page. These decisions require higher-order thinking skills, such as analysis, synthesis, and evaluation. Drawing also demands the integration of sensory input (such as visual perception) with motor output (the control of hand movements). The process of visually examining an object or scene and translating it onto paper involves several brain regions, including the occipital lobe (responsible for visual processing) and the parietal lobe (involved in spatial reasoning and motor coordination).

Beyond the technical aspects, drawing encourages creative problem-solving. Artists often experiment with different techniques, materials, and approaches to achieve their desired results. This experimentation fosters cognitive flexibility, which is the ability to switch between different ways of thinking or approaches to a problem. The prefrontal cortex, which is involved in decision-making, planning, and regulating attention, plays a key role in managing the complex cognitive demands of drawing. As individuals practice drawing, they become better at evaluating different options and selecting the most effective strategies for achieving their artistic goals.

Painting, like drawing, stimulates thought processes by requiring the artist to make decisions about composition, color, texture, and perspective. However, painting introduces additional cognitive challenges, such as understanding color theory and manipulating materials like paint, brushes, and canvas. These added elements demand a higher level of conceptual thinking. When choosing and mixing colors, for instance, artists must understand how different hues interact with one another, how to create contrast or harmony, and how colors evoke emotions. This process requires abstract thinking because it involves understanding relationships between non-physical qualities (such as how certain colors can convey a particular mood or atmosphere).

Moreover, painting encourages emotional expression and the development of empathy. Artists often use painting as a way to express feelings that may be difficult to articulate verbally. By translating emotions into visual forms, individuals can process and understand their feelings more deeply. This form of emotional engagement also activates the limbic system, the part of the brain involved in emotional regulation and memory. In this way, painting serves as a bridge between cognitive and emotional development, helping individuals refine their emotional intelligence alongside their creative thinking skills.

Sculpting, the process of creating three-dimensional forms, introduces a different set of cognitive challenges that further enhance mental development. Sculpting requires a deep understanding of spatial relationships, as the artist must work with physical materials and manipulate them in three dimensions. This process involves spatial reasoning, a cognitive skill that allows individuals to visualize objects from different perspectives, predict how they will look when manipulated, and plan the steps needed to achieve a desired form.

Sculpting also engages the motor cortex, which controls voluntary muscle movements, as well as the parietal lobe, which integrates sensory information to guide hand movements. The tactile nature of sculpting, where individuals work directly with materials such as clay, wood, or metal, engages the sense of touch and enhances sensory processing. This multi sensory experience helps individuals develop a more refined understanding of their environment and how different objects interact with one another.

In addition to the physical and spatial demands of sculpting, the process encourages problem-solving and creativity. Sculptors must think critically about how to achieve their desired forms, often experimenting with different techniques and materials to overcome challenges. This process of trial and error promotes cognitive resilience, the ability to persist in the face of difficulties and continue seeking solutions. Cognitive resilience is a key component of cognitive growth, as it enables individuals to approach complex tasks with confidence and flexibility.

All three forms of visual art—drawing, painting, and sculpting—stimulate thought processes by engaging multiple brain regions, encouraging critical thinking, and promoting problem-solving. These activities provide a platform for individuals to explore their creativity, develop new ideas, and refine their understanding of the world around them.

Visual Memory and Spatial Awareness

Visual memory is the ability to remember visual information, such as shapes, colors, and patterns. It plays a crucial role in cognitive development because it allows individuals to retain and recall important details from their environment. Spatial awareness, on the other hand, refers to the ability to understand and navigate the relationships between objects in space. Both visual memory and spatial awareness are essential for a wide range of cognitive tasks, including reading, writing, mathematics, and problem-solving.

Engaging in visual arts, such as drawing, painting, and sculpting, enhances visual memory by requiring individuals to pay close attention to details and remember the visual elements of their subject. For example, when an artist draws or paints a landscape, they must recall the shapes, colors, and proportions of the objects in the scene. This process strengthens the neural connections involved in visual memory, particularly in the occipital and temporal lobes, which are responsible for processing and storing visual information.

Research has shown that individuals who regularly engage in visual arts tend to have better visual memory than those who do not. This is because artistic activities require continuous practice in observing, remembering, and replicating visual details. As a result, artists develop a heightened ability to recall visual information, which can benefit them in other areas of life, such as academic learning or problem-solving.

Spatial awareness is another cognitive skill that is closely linked to visual arts. When individuals engage in activities such as drawing or sculpting, they must constantly consider the spatial relationships between objects. For example, when drawing a portrait, an artist must think about the proportions of the face, the positioning of the features, and how they relate to one another in space. Similarly, when sculpting, the artist must consider how different parts of the sculpture will interact with one another and how the overall form will take shape.

This focus on spatial relationships enhances spatial reasoning, a cognitive skill that allows individuals to visualize objects in space and understand how they relate to one another. Spatial reasoning is essential for many everyday tasks, such as navigating through a city, assembling furniture, or solving puzzles. It is also a critical component of STEM (science, technology, engineering, and mathematics) education, where students are often required to understand complex spatial concepts, such as geometry, physics, and engineering design.

Visual arts provide an excellent platform for developing spatial reasoning skills because they require individuals to think about objects in three dimensions and understand how different elements interact in space. Studies have shown that individuals who engage in activities that promote spatial awareness, such as drawing or sculpting, tend to perform better in tasks that require spatial reasoning, such as solving puzzles or understanding mathematical concepts.

In addition to enhancing spatial reasoning, engaging in visual arts also promotes cognitive mapping, which is the ability to create mental representations of one's environment. Cognitive mapping is essential for navigation and spatial orientation, allowing individuals to understand the layout of their surroundings and find their way from one place to another. Artistic activities, particularly those that involve creating landscapes or cityscapes, encourage individuals to develop cognitive maps by requiring them to visualize and represent complex spatial relationships.

The development of visual memory and spatial awareness through visual arts has long-term benefits for cognitive growth. These skills are essential for academic success, particularly in subjects such as mathematics, science, and engineering, where spatial reasoning and memory play a crucial role. Moreover, the ability to visualize and remember complex patterns and relationships is critical for problem-solving and creative thinking, both of which are essential for success in a wide range of fields.

The Connection Between Fine Motor Skills and Cognitive Growth

Fine motor skills refer to the ability to control small muscle movements, particularly those involving the hands and fingers. These skills are essential for tasks such as writing, drawing, cutting, and manipulating objects. Fine motor skills are closely linked to cognitive growth because they require the brain to coordinate sensory input with precise motor output. Engaging in activities that promote fine motor skills, such as drawing, painting, and sculpting, not only enhances physical coordination but also stimulates brain development.

When individuals engage in visual arts, they must use their hands and fingers to manipulate tools such as pencils, brushes, or sculpting tools. This process requires the integration of sensory information (such as visual and tactile feedback) with motor commands, allowing the brain to fine-tune its control over the muscles involved in the activity. This integration occurs in the motor cortex, which is responsible for controlling voluntary movements, as well as the cerebellum, which helps coordinate and refine these movements.

The development of fine motor skills through visual arts is particularly important during early childhood, a critical period for brain development. As children practice drawing, painting, or sculpting, they strengthen the neural connections involved in motor control, enhancing their ability to perform precise and coordinated movements. These improvements in fine motor skills have broader cognitive benefits because they allow children to engage more effectively in academic tasks such as writing or using tools in science experiments.

Research has shown that children who regularly engage in visual arts activities, which require fine motor skills, tend to perform better in tasks that require precision, attention to detail, and hand-eye coordination. For example, children who practice drawing or painting often develop better handwriting skills because they have refined their ability to control the small muscles in their hands and fingers. These improvements in fine motor skills extend beyond artistic activities and support other areas of academic and cognitive development, such as reading, mathematics, and science.

One of the key reasons why fine motor skills are so closely linked to cognitive growth is that they require the brain to engage in bimanual coordination, which involves using both hands together to complete a task. Bimanual coordination activates both hemispheres of the brain, encouraging communication between the left and right hemispheres through the corpus callosum, a bundle of nerve fibers that connects the two sides of the brain. This interhemispheric communication is essential for integrating sensory and motor information and for executing coordinated movements.

For instance, when a child is sculpting with clay, they may use one hand to hold the clay steady while the other hand shapes it. This process requires the brain to coordinate the movements of both hands, enhancing the development of fine motor control. Over time, these experiences strengthen the brain's ability to manage complex motor tasks and integrate them with cognitive processes such as spatial reasoning and problem-solving.

In addition to promoting bimanual coordination, engaging in visual arts also enhances hand-eye coordination, which is the ability to control hand movements in response to visual stimuli. Hand-eye coordination is crucial for many everyday tasks, such as catching a ball, typing on a keyboard, or using tools. In the context of visual arts, hand-eye coordination is essential for translating visual information (such as the shape and position of an object) into precise motor actions (such as drawing a line or shaping a piece of clay).

The development of hand-eye coordination through visual arts has significant cognitive benefits. For example, children who practice drawing or painting learn to synchronize their hand movements with their visual perceptions, improving their ability to perform tasks that require both precision and accuracy. This enhanced coordination supports broader cognitive functions such as attention, concentration, and working memory, all of which are essential for academic success.

Moreover, the process of developing fine motor skills through visual arts encourages problem-solving and executive function. When children engage in activities such as drawing, painting, or sculpting, they often encounter challenges that require them to think critically and devise solutions. For example, a child sculpting a figure out of clay may need to adjust the pressure they apply or modify the shape of the material to achieve their desired result. This process of trial and error promotes cognitive flexibility, as children learn to adapt their approach based on the feedback they receive from their environment.

Fine motor skills development also supports goal-directed behavior, which is the ability to set and work toward specific objectives. Artistic activities often involve setting a goal (such as completing a drawing or creating a sculpture) and taking the necessary steps to achieve it. This process helps children develop self-regulation and perseverance, as they learn to stay focused on a task, manage frustration, and make adjustments as needed. These executive function skills are critical for cognitive growth, as they enable individuals to plan, organize, and execute complex tasks in both academic and non-academic contexts.

The connection between fine motor skills and cognitive growth is also evident in the way that these skills contribute to the development of working memory. Working memory refers to the brain's ability to hold and manipulate information in real time, and it plays a crucial role in tasks such as problem-solving, decision-making, and learning. Engaging in activities that require fine motor skills, such as drawing or painting, challenges individuals to hold multiple pieces of information in their working memory, such as the size, shape, and position of the object they are creating.

For example, when a child is drawing a house, they must remember the overall shape of the house while also attending to the details of the windows, doors, and roof. This process of holding and manipulating multiple pieces of information strengthens the neural circuits involved in working memory, enhancing the child's ability to perform other cognitive tasks that require attention and concentration.

In addition to its impact on working memory, fine motor skills development also contributes to long-term memory by reinforcing the neural pathways involved in learning and retention. Repetitive practice of fine motor tasks, such as drawing or sculpting, helps consolidate information in long-term memory, allowing individuals to retrieve it more easily in the future. This process is particularly important for academic learning, where the ability to retain and recall information is essential for success.

The cognitive benefits of fine motor skills development are not limited to childhood. Adults who engage in visual arts activities that require fine motor skills, such as painting or sculpting, also experience improvements in cognitive function, particularly in areas such as attention, memory, and problem-solving. Research has shown that older adults who regularly engage in creative activities tend to have better cognitive health and a lower risk of cognitive decline. By continuing to practice fine motor skills throughout life, individuals can maintain and even enhance their cognitive abilities, contributing to lifelong learning and mental agility.

In educational settings, incorporating visual arts activities that promote fine motor skills development can have a significant impact on students' cognitive growth and academic performance. Studies have shown that children who participate in arts education tend to perform better in subjects such as reading, writing, and mathematics. This is because the cognitive skills developed through artistic expression, such as attention to detail, spatial reasoning, and hand-eye coordination, transfer to other academic domains. By fostering fine motor skills through visual arts, educators can help students develop the intellectual tools they need to succeed in school and beyond.

In conclusion, the development of fine motor skills through visual arts plays a critical role in cognitive growth. By engaging in activities such as drawing, painting, and sculpting, individuals not only enhance their physical coordination but also stimulate a wide range of cognitive processes, including problem-solving, memory, attention, and executive function. These cognitive benefits extend beyond artistic activities and contribute to overall intellectual development, supporting success in academic and everyday tasks. As such, promoting fine motor skills development through visual arts is an essential component of fostering cognitive growth and lifelong learning.

Music and Cognitive Enhancement

Music has long been considered an enriching component of human life, capable of evoking powerful emotions and creating deep connections. However, beyond its cultural and emotional significance, music plays a significant role in cognitive development and enhancement. Scientific research has uncovered the profound effects that music can have on various aspects of cognitive functioning, including memory, problem-solving, and overall brain development. By understanding how music influences the brain, we can better appreciate its potential as a tool for enhancing learning and cognitive growth.

The Effects of Music on Memory and Problem-Solving

Memory is one of the most studied areas in the relationship between music and cognitive enhancement. Numerous studies have demonstrated that music, particularly certain types of structured music, can improve both short-term and long-term memory. The interaction between music and memory lies in how music affects various brain regions involved in memory formation, retention, and retrieval. These include the hippocampus, a critical structure for memory consolidation, and the prefrontal cortex, which is involved in working memory and decision-making processes.

Music is thought to aid memory through a process known as encoding, where information is organized and stored in the brain in a more structured and accessible way. When individuals listen to music, the rhythmic and repetitive nature of the sounds can create cues that help encode and later retrieve information. For instance, when students listen to music while studying, they may associate specific pieces of information with certain rhythms or melodies, making it easier to recall the information later.

This phenomenon is most apparent in musical mnemonics, a technique that uses music to help individuals remember information. Mnemonics that incorporate music have been used for centuries, particularly in educational settings. Think of how young children learn the alphabet through the ABC song or how historical events are often taught through rhythm and rhyme. Music's structured and repetitive nature helps break down complex information into manageable chunks, allowing for easier retrieval from memory.

Beyond aiding in simple recall, music has been shown to improve working memory, which is crucial for problem-solving and decision-making. Working memory refers to the brain's ability to hold and manipulate information for short periods while performing cognitive tasks. Research has shown that individuals who engage with music regularly—whether through listening, singing, or playing an instrument—often demonstrate superior working memory capabilities. This is particularly evident in musicians, who need to remember complex sequences of notes, rhythms, and harmonies while simultaneously executing their performance.

Music training, particularly at an early age, has been associated with enhancements in working memory. In musicians, this is seen in their ability to maintain multiple auditory patterns in mind while reading sheet music, performing motor tasks, and making real-time decisions. This heightened working memory capacity extends beyond musical tasks and translates into other areas of life, such as academic achievement, where individuals need to retain and manipulate information across various disciplines.

Problem-solving is another cognitive area in which music plays a significant role. Problem-solving requires creativity, critical thinking, and the ability to integrate various types of information into coherent solutions. The act of listening to or creating music engages multiple brain regions that contribute to these functions. For example, playing an instrument requires real-time coordination between the motor cortex, which controls fine motor skills, and the prefrontal cortex, which is responsible for planning and decision-making. In addition, the auditory cortex processes the sounds, while the parietal lobe helps with spatial awareness—essential when reading music or understanding complex musical structures.

Music's influence on problem-solving is closely linked to its ability to enhance cognitive flexibility, or the capacity to switch between different thought processes. Listening to or performing music often involves recognizing patterns, shifting between different musical themes, and adjusting one's thinking in response to changes in rhythm or melody. This type of flexibility is crucial for solving problems that require adaptive thinking, such as puzzles, mathematical challenges, or strategic games.

Moreover, music encourages divergent thinking, which is the process of generating multiple potential solutions to a problem rather than focusing on a single, predetermined solution. This form of thinking is essential for creative problem-solving and innovation. Studies have shown that individuals who engage with music, particularly through improvisation or composing, tend to demonstrate higher levels of divergent thinking compared to those who do not regularly engage in musical activities.

Rhythm, Pattern Recognition, and Brain Development

Rhythm is one of the most fundamental elements of music and plays a critical role in cognitive development. The human brain is naturally wired to recognize patterns, and rhythmic patterns in music provide a structured framework that the brain can easily process and understand. This ability to perceive and predict rhythmic patterns is not only crucial for musical cognition but also for a wide range of cognitive tasks, including language acquisition, reading comprehension, and mathematical reasoning.

Pattern recognition is a cognitive process that allows individuals to identify regularities in their environment, whether they are visual, auditory, or spatial. In music, pattern recognition involves identifying recurring rhythms, melodies, or harmonies and understanding how these elements fit together to form a cohesive whole. This process engages brain regions such as the auditory cortex, which processes sound, and the prefrontal cortex, which helps organize and interpret these patterns.

The brain's ability to recognize and predict patterns in music is closely linked to its development of executive functions, which include skills such as planning, organizing, and problem-solving. As individuals listen to music, they unconsciously predict upcoming rhythmic or melodic patterns based on their previous experience with similar music. This process of anticipation and prediction is crucial for developing executive functions, as it allows individuals to plan ahead, make decisions, and adjust their behavior based on changing circumstances.

Rhythm, in particular, plays a significant role in temporal processing, which refers to the brain's ability to understand and manage the passage of time. Temporal processing is essential for many cognitive tasks, including under-standing speech, coordinating movement, and solving problems. Research has shown that individuals who have a strong sense of rhythm tend to perform better on tasks that require precise timing and coordination, such as playing sports, dancing, or performing complex motor tasks.

Moreover, rhythm is closely tied to the development of language skills. Language, like music, is structured around rhythmic patterns, with spoken language consisting of syllables, words, and phrases that follow predictable rhythmic structures. Infants and young children are particularly sensitive to rhythm, and their ability to recognize and respond to rhythmic patterns in speech is essential for language acquisition. Studies have shown that children who are exposed to music and rhythm-based activities at an early age tend to develop stronger language skills, including better phonological awareness (the ability to recognize and manipulate sounds in speech) and improved reading comprehension.

Brain development is heavily influenced by exposure to rhythmic and patterned activities such as music. Neuroscientific research has demonstrated that music, particularly rhythm, promotes neuroplasticity, which is the brain's ability to reorganize and form new neural connections in response to learning and experience. This process of neuroplasticity is particularly pronounced during early childhood, when the brain is most receptive to external stimuli.

When children engage in musical activities that involve rhythm, such as clapping, drumming, or dancing, they stimulate multiple areas of the brain involved in auditory processing, motor control, and sensory integration. These activities strengthen the neural pathways that connect these brain regions, enhancing the brain's overall connectivity and efficiency. Over time, this improved connectivity contributes to enhanced cognitive functions such as memory, attention, and problem-solving.

In addition to its impact on brain connectivity, rhythm-based activities promote the development of motor skills and coordination. Playing an instrument or participating in rhythm-based activities requires precise timing and coordination between different muscle groups. This process engages the cerebellum, which is responsible for motor control, as well as the motor cortex, which coordinates voluntary muscle movements. The development of these motor skills has broader cognitive benefits, as it supports the brain's ability to perform complex tasks that require both physical and mental coordination.

Furthermore, rhythm-based activities have been shown to improve attention and focus, particularly in children with attention deficit hyperactivity disorder (ADHD). Research has shown that rhythmic training, such as drumming or clapping to a steady beat, can help children with ADHD improve their ability to sustain attention and regulate their impulses. This is because rhythm provides a structured and predictable framework that helps individuals focus their attention and organize their thoughts. Over time, regular engagement with rhythm-based activities can lead to improvements in overall attention span and cognitive control.

Case Studies: Music as a Tool for Learning

Numerous case studies and research projects have demonstrated the potential of music as a tool for enhancing learning and cognitive development. These case studies highlight how music can be integrated into educational settings to improve academic performance, foster creativity, and support the development of essential cognitive skills.

One notable case study involved a group of elementary school students who participated in a music education program designed to enhance their reading and language skills. The program, which included activities such as singing, rhythm-based exercises, and instrumental practice, was implemented alongside the students' regular academic curriculum. After several months of participation in the program, the students demonstrated significant improvements in their reading comprehension and phonological awareness compared to a control group that did not receive music instruction.

The researchers attributed these improvements to the cognitive overlap between music and language skills. Both music and language involve the processing of sound, rhythm, and patterns, and the skills developed through music instruction—such as recognizing rhythmic patterns, identifying changes in pitch, and maintaining attention—are directly applicable to language learning. This case study underscores the potential of music education to enhance academic performance, particularly in areas related to literacy and language development.

Another case study focused on the use of music to improve mathematical reasoning in middle school students. The study involved a group of students who participated in a music-based math intervention program, where they learned to apply musical concepts such as rhythm, pattern recognition, and sequencing to mathematical problem-solving. The program included activities such as composing rhythmic patterns to represent mathematical equations and using musical notation to understand mathematical sequences. Over time, the students demonstrated significant improvements in their mathematical reasoning and problem-solving abilities compared to a control group that received traditional math instruction without the integration of music.

The connection between music and mathematics lies in the shared cognitive processes involved in both disciplines. Both music and mathematics require the recognition of patterns, the understanding of sequences, and the ability to manipulate abstract symbols. The rhythmic and structured nature of music helps students develop their ability to organize information logically, which translates directly to improved mathematical problem-solving. This case study highlights the potential of using music as a tool to enhance mathematical learning by engaging students in an enjoyable and cognitively stimulating activity.

Music has also been successfully used as a tool for emotional regulation and social learning, particularly in students with special educational needs. One case study involved a group of children with autism spectrum disorder (ASD) who participated in a music therapy program aimed at improving their social communication skills. The program included activities such as singing, playing instruments, and engaging in musical improvisation, all of which were designed to encourage social interaction and emotional expression.

The results of the study were remarkable: the children who participated in the music therapy program showed significant improvements in their ability to engage in social interactions, maintain eye contact, and express their emotions through both verbal and non-verbal means. Music provided a non-threatening and structured environment in which the children could practice social communication skills in a way that felt natural and enjoyable. The researchers concluded that music therapy can be an effective tool for enhancing the social and emotional development of children with ASD by providing a medium through which they can connect with others and express themselves.

Additionally, music has been used as a memory aid for individuals with Alzheimer's disease and dementia, demonstrating its profound effects on long-term memory retrieval. In one case study, elderly patients with Alzheimer's disease were introduced to a music-based reminiscence therapy program, where they listened to songs from their past while engaging in discussions about their personal memories associated with the music. The program was designed to stimulate memory recall by using music as a trigger for accessing long-term memories.

The results of the study showed that the patients who participated in the music-based reminiscence therapy demonstrated significant improvements in their ability to recall personal memories, even when other forms of memory stimulation had proven ineffective. Music seemed to activate neural pathways that allowed the patients to access memories that had been otherwise inaccessible. This case study highlights the potential of music as a therapeutic tool for individuals with memory impairments, suggesting that music can provide a powerful means of unlocking long-term memories and enhancing cognitive function in older adults.

In educational settings, music has also been used to improve focus and attention in students with attention difficulties, such as those with ADHD. One case study involved a group of students with ADHD who participated in a rhythmic entertainment program, where they practiced clapping, drumming, and moving to a steady beat. The goal of the program was to help the students develop better impulse control and attention regulation by training their brains to follow rhythmic patterns.

After several weeks of participation in the program, the students demon-strated significant improvements in their ability to sustain attention and complete tasks in the classroom. The rhythmic training seemed to help the students regulate their attention by providing a predictable and structured framework that supported cognitive control. This case study suggests that rhythmic entertainment and music-based interventions can be effective tools for improving attention and focus in students with attention difficulties, offering an alternative approach to traditional behavioral interventions.

In conclusion, music is a powerful tool for enhancing cognitive development across various domains, including memory, problem-solving, language ac-quisition, mathematical reasoning, emotional regulation, and social learning. Case studies from educational and therapeutic settings have demonstrated the profound impact that music can have on individuals' cognitive functioning, providing compelling evidence for the integration of music into both academic curricula and therapeutic interventions. By understanding the effects of music on the brain and incorporating music-based activities into learning and development, we can unlock the full potential of cognitive enhancement through music.

Dance and Movement: Connecting Body and Mind

D ance and movement have been integral to human culture and development for millennia. Beyond their social and cultural significance, dance and movement offer profound cognitive, emotional, and physical benefits. The study of kinesthetic learning, which focuses on how physical movement can enhance cognitive processes, reveals that bodily engagement is crucial for brain development and learning. When individuals dance or engage in rhythmic movement, they activate various brain regions responsible for motor coordination, spatial awareness, and emotional regulation. This chapter explores how dance and movement serve as powerful tools for enhancing cognitive functions, promoting emotional well-being, and developing essential skills related to coordination and spatial understanding.

Kinesthetic Learning and Cognitive Benefits

Kinesthetic learning refers to the process of acquiring knowledge through physical movement. This type of learning is especially important for individuals who learn best by doing rather than by observing or listening. For many, physical movement facilitates deeper understanding of complex concepts, making kinesthetic learning a valuable educational tool. Dance, as a form of kinesthetic learning, encourages participants to actively engage their bodies in ways that stimulate both the brain and the body, promoting cognitive development and enhancing memory, attention, and creativity.

The cognitive benefits of dance are rooted in how the brain processes and integrates sensory and motor information. When people dance, they must coordinate their movements with music, remember complex choreographic sequences, and adjust their motions based on their environment and partners. These tasks require the simultaneous activation of various brain regions, including the motor cortex, which controls voluntary movement, and the cerebellum, which coordinates balance and motor precision. Furthermore, the prefrontal cortex, responsible for executive function and decision-making, is heavily involved in processing movement sequences and adapting to the demands of a dance routine.

One of the most notable cognitive benefits of kinesthetic learning through dance is its ability to enhance memory. Dance requires participants to remember intricate sequences of steps, spatial patterns, and rhythmic timing. These aspects of dance tap into procedural memory, a type of long-term memory involved in learning motor tasks, and working memory, which is necessary for holding and manipulating information in real-time. Repeating these movements helps to solidify the connections between neurons involved in memory retrieval and motor skills.

In addition to enhancing memory, dance promotes problem-solving skills. Choreography often requires dancers to solve spatial and temporal challenges, such as how to navigate across the floor, avoid collisions with other dancers, and coordinate movements with music. Dancers must also adapt their movements in response to the tempo of the music or the dynamics of their partners. This process of adjusting to new challenges fosters cognitive flexibility, which is the ability to switch between different mental tasks and adapt to changing circumstances. Cognitive flexibility is essential for problem-solving in various aspects of life, as it enables individuals to approach challenges from multiple perspectives and devise creative solutions.

Dance also improves focus and attention, as it requires sustained concentration to perform sequences accurately. When dancing, individuals must pay close attention to their body's position, their surroundings, and the timing of their movements. This level of attentiveness activates the parietal lobes, which are involved in spatial awareness and attention control. Over time, practicing dance helps to strengthen the brain's ability to focus on specific tasks and block out distractions, leading to improvements in sustained attention both on and off the dance floor.

Creativity is another cognitive area that is enhanced through dance. Whether dancers are improvising movements or interpreting choreography, they are constantly generating new ideas and experimenting with different ways of expressing themselves. This process of creative exploration engages the default mode network (DMN), a brain network associated with daydreaming, imagination, and divergent thinking. By fostering creativity through movement, dance encourages individuals to think outside the box and develop new ways of approaching problems, whether in their personal, academic, or professional lives.

Kinesthetic learning also plays a role in promoting embodied cognition, a theory that suggests that cognitive processes are deeply rooted in the body's interactions with the world. According to this theory, physical movement and sensory experiences shape the way we think and understand concepts. Dance, as a form of embodied cognition, allows individuals to physically engage with abstract ideas, such as rhythm, balance, and emotion. For example, a dancer interpreting a piece of music may use their body to express the mood or narrative of the composition, translating auditory information into a physical form. This process of embodying abstract concepts helps to reinforce understanding and retention of those ideas.

In educational settings, incorporating kinesthetic learning through dance and movement can have significant cognitive benefits for students. Research has shown that students who participate in movement-based learning activities tend to perform better in subjects such as mathematics, reading, and science. This is because dance engages multiple cognitive processes, such as memory, attention, and problem-solving, which are essential for academic success. By integrating dance into the curriculum, educators can help students develop their cognitive skills while also promoting physical health and emotional well-being.

The Importance of Dance for Spatial Awareness and Motor Coordination

Spatial awareness is the ability to understand and navigate the spatial relationships between objects in an environment. It involves recognizing where one's body is in space and how to move efficiently within that space. Motor coordination refers to the ability to control and synchronize movements in a smooth and purposeful manner. Both spatial awareness and motor coordination are essential for a wide range of everyday activities, from walking and driving to playing sports and interacting with others.

Dance is one of the most effective ways to develop spatial awareness and motor coordination, as it requires participants to move their bodies in precise and controlled ways while navigating through space. When individuals dance, they must be aware of their body's position relative to the floor, other dancers, and their environment. This constant awareness of spatial relationships engages the parietal lobes, which are responsible for processing spatial information, and the cerebellum, which coordinates movement and balance.

In dance, spatial awareness is particularly important for understanding proxemics, or the use of space in social interactions. Dancers must be mindful of their proximity to others, adjusting their movements to avoid collisions and maintain proper spacing within a group. This skill is not only essential for dance but also for everyday social interactions, as it helps individuals navigate crowded environments, maintain personal space, and interact smoothly with others.

Motor coordination is another critical aspect of dance that contributes to cognitive and physical development. Dance requires the precise coordination of multiple muscle groups to perform complex movements, such as spins, jumps, and footwork. This level of coordination engages the motor cortex, which controls voluntary movement, and the basal ganglia, which helps refine motor control and smooth out movement sequences.

The development of motor coordination through dance has broader implications for cognitive growth. Research has shown that individuals with strong motor coordination tend to perform better in tasks that require executive function, such as planning, organizing, and multitasking. This is because motor coordination helps to strengthen the brain's ability to control and regulate movement, which is closely linked to the brain's capacity for cognitive control. For example, a dancer who can precisely coordinate their movements to music is also likely to excel in tasks that require precise timing, attention to detail, and the ability to switch between different tasks.

Moreover, dance enhances balance and proprioception, which is the body's ability to sense its position and movement in space. Balance is essential for performing many types of dance movements, from simple steps to more advanced choreography involving jumps and turns. Proprioception, on the other hand, helps dancers understand how their body is positioned in space and how to adjust their movements accordingly. Both balance and proprioception are critical for maintaining motor coordination and avoiding injury, both in dance and in everyday activities.

The development of spatial awareness and motor coordination through dance has significant cognitive benefits beyond the dance floor. For example, individuals with strong spatial awareness tend to perform better in tasks that require spatial reasoning, such as navigating through a city, assembling furniture, or solving puzzles. Similarly, individuals with well-developed motor coordination are more likely to excel in tasks that require fine motor skills, such as writing, typing, or playing a musical instrument.

In educational settings, incorporating dance into physical education programs can help students develop their spatial awareness and motor coordination while also promoting cognitive growth. Studies have shown that students who participate in dance-based physical education programs tend to demonstrate better motor skills, improved balance, and enhanced spatial reasoning compared to students who engage in more traditional forms of physical exercise. By fostering spatial awareness and motor coordination through dance, educators can help students develop the cognitive and physical skills they need to succeed in both academic and everyday life.

The Emotional and Cognitive Benefits of Dance

In addition to its cognitive and physical benefits, dance also offers significant emotional and psychological advantages. Dance provides a powerful outlet for emotional expression, allowing individuals to process and communicate their feelings in a non-verbal way. Whether through structured choreography or free form improvisation, dance enables individuals to connect with their emotions and express them in ways that words often cannot capture. This form of emotional expression is essential for emotional regulation, which refers to the ability to manage and control one's emotions in response to different situations.

When individuals engage in dance, they often experience a release of dopamine and endorphins, neurotransmitters associated with pleasure, reward, and stress relief. These neurochemical changes contribute to the sense of joy, relaxation, and well-being that many people experience during and after dancing. Dance can serve as an effective form of stress reduction, helping individuals manage anxiety, depression, and other emotional challenges. The combination of physical movement and emotional expression in dance allows individuals to release pent-up emotions and process their feelings in a healthy and constructive way.

Moreover, dance fosters empathy and social connection. When individuals dance in a group or with a partner, they must pay attention to the emotions and movements of others, adjusting their own movements to synchronize with the group. This process of attuning to others' emotional and physical cues helps to strengthen social cognition, the ability to understand and respond to the thoughts, feelings, and actions of others. Social cognition is crucial for empathy and emotional intelligence, and dance provides a unique environment in which these skills can be developed and refined.

One of the reasons dance is so effective in fostering empathy is that it requires individuals to engage in mirroring, a process in which dancers imitate each other's movements. This physical mimicry is not just about copying movements; it involves deeply understanding and feeling the emotions behind the actions. For example, when two dancers mirror each other's steps, they are also mirroring the emotional intent behind those movements, whether it's joy, sadness, or tension. This form of non-verbal communication enhances emotional atonement and helps individuals become more empathetic and responsive to the emotional states of others.

In therapeutic settings, dance has been used as a tool for emotional healing and self-expression. Dance therapy, also known as dance/movement therapy (DMT), is an evidence-based practice that uses movement to promote emotional, cognitive, and physical integration. It has been particularly effective in helping individuals with trauma, depression, and anxiety. For those who find it difficult to articulate their emotions verbally, dance provides an alternative way to express and process deep-seated emotions. The act of moving one's body in response to emotions can lead to breakthroughs in emotional understanding and regulation.

Furthermore, the emotional benefits of dance extend to its ability to enhance self-esteem and body image. For many, the act of dancing—whether alone or in a group—provides a sense of accomplishment and pride in their physical abilities. This is especially important for individuals who may struggle with self-confidence or negative perceptions of their body. Through dance, individuals learn to appreciate their bodies for what they can do, rather than focusing on how they look. This shift in perspective fosters a healthier relationship with one's body and can improve overall self-esteem and body image.

From a cognitive perspective, the emotional regulation that dance fosters has direct implications for cognitive performance. When individuals are able to manage their emotions effectively, they are better able to focus, think critically, and make decisions. Emotional regulation enhances executive function, allowing individuals to stay calm and focused during challenging cognitive tasks. For example, a dancer who has learned to manage stage fright or performance anxiety through emotional regulation techniques will be better equipped to handle stressful academic or work-related challenges. The emotional resilience gained through dance translates into improved cognitive flexibility and problem-solving skills.

The emotional and cognitive benefits of dance are also evident in creative expression. Dance encourages individuals to experiment with new movements, rhythms, and patterns, fostering creative thinking and innovation. Whether through improvisation or choreography, dancers constantly explore new ways to move their bodies, which requires them to think creatively and adapt to new challenges. This process of creative exploration is closely linked to divergent thinking, the ability to generate multiple possible solutions to a problem. Divergent thinking is essential for creativity and innovation in all areas of life, from artistic endeavors to problem-solving in professional settings.

Creative expression in dance also engages the brain's default mode network (DMN), which is active during moments of introspection, imagination, and daydreaming. This brain network is critical for creative thinking, as it allows individuals to explore new ideas and possibilities without the constraints of immediate tasks or goals. When dancers engage in improvisation, they tap into the DMN to generate new movements and ideas, which helps to enhance their overall creativity and cognitive flexibility. This creative process is not only fulfilling on an emotional level but also promotes cognitive growth by encouraging individuals to think in new and innovative ways.

Moreover, dance enhances emotional intelligence, which is the ability to recognize, understand, and manage one's own emotions as well as the emotions of others. Emotional intelligence is critical for success in both personal and professional life, as it allows individuals to navigate social interactions, resolve conflicts, and build strong relationships. Dance provides an ideal environment for developing emotional intelligence because it involves constant interaction with others and requires individuals to be attuned to the emotional tone of their movements and the movements of those around them.

The combination of emotional expression, social interaction, and physical movement in dance makes it a powerful tool for enhancing emotional intelligence. For example, in partner dance styles such as salsa or tango, dancers must be highly attuned to their partner's movements and emotions to maintain synchronization and flow. This atonement requires both empathy and emotional regulation, as dancers must respond to their partner's emotional cues while managing their own emotional state. Over time, these skills become more refined, leading to improvements in emotional intelligence that extend beyond the dance floor.

In addition to its role in enhancing emotional intelligence, dance also fosters social connection and community building. Many forms of dance, from traditional folk dances to modern hip-hop, are inherently social activities that bring people together in a shared experience. This sense of community and connection is particularly important in a world where individuals are often isolated by technology and busy schedules. Dance provides a space for individuals to connect with others on a deeper level, building trust, cooperation, and a sense of belonging.

Research has shown that participating in group dance activities can lead to increased feelings of social disconnectedness and group cohesion. When individuals dance together, they often experience a phenomenon known as entertainment, where their movements and physiological rhythms (such as heart rate and breathing) become synchronized with those of the other dancers. This synchronization fosters a sense of unity and collective purpose, which can strengthen social bonds and create a sense of community.

In therapeutic contexts, dance has been used to help individuals build social skills and develop healthier relationships. For individuals with social anxiety, for example, dance provides a structured and supportive environment in which they can practice interacting with others in a non-verbal way. This can help reduce feelings of social isolation and increase confidence in social situations. Similarly, dance has been used in rehabilitation programs for individuals recovering from trauma or addiction, as it provides a positive outlet for emotional expression and helps individuals rebuild their sense of self and their connections to others.

In educational settings, incorporating dance into the curriculum can help students develop both their emotional and cognitive skills. Studies have shown that students who participate in dance programs tend to have better emotional regulation, higher self-esteem, and improved social skills compared to those who do not engage in dance. These emotional benefits, in turn, enhance cognitive performance by reducing stress, improving focus, and fostering a positive attitude toward learning.

In conclusion, dance offers a unique combination of cognitive, emotional, and social benefits that make it a powerful tool for personal growth and development. By engaging in dance, individuals not only enhance their spatial awareness, motor coordination, and cognitive flexibility but also improve their emotional regulation, empathy, and social disconnectedness. The emotional and cognitive benefits of dance extend beyond the dance floor, contributing to success in academic, professional, and personal life. As such, dance should be recognized as a valuable and holistic form of learning that connects the body and mind in profound and meaningful ways.

Drama and Role-Playing in Cognitive and Emotional Development

D rama and role-playing have long been recognized as powerful tools for both cognitive and emotional development, offering individuals the opportunity to engage in creative expression, explore different perspectives, and practice social interaction in a safe and structured environment. By stepping into the roles of different characters, individuals can experience situations outside their own lives, allowing them to gain empathy, develop social skills, and refine their emotional intelligence. Role-playing and storytelling are not merely recreational activities; they have profound implications for cognitive processes such as critical thinking, problem-solving, and emotional regulation. This chapter delves into the ways in which drama and role-playing contribute to both cognitive and emotional growth.

Enhancing Empathy and Social Skills through Role-Playing

Empathy, the ability to understand and share the feelings of others, is a critical component of emotional intelligence and social interaction. Role-playing, particularly in a dramatic context, provides a structured and imaginative way for individuals to develop empathy by stepping into the shoes of another person. Whether it's in the context of theater, therapeutic role-playing, or educational drama activities, participants are required to imagine the thoughts, feelings, and motivations of their characters. This process of perspective-taking allows individuals to practice emotional atonement and understanding, which enhances their capacity for empathy in real-life situations.

Role-playing requires individuals to go beyond their own subjective experiences and consider how someone else might perceive and respond to a situation. For example, in a dramatic exercise where a participant takes on the role of a person facing a difficult moral decision, they must grapple with the emotions and conflicts inherent in that scenario. This ability to adopt different perspectives is a cornerstone of empathy, as it allows individuals to better understand the emotional experiences of others. As participants practice this skill in a controlled environment, they become more adept at applying it in their everyday interactions, leading to improved relationships and social cohesion.

The development of empathy through role-playing is particularly significant for children and adolescents, who are still in the process of refining their social and emotional skills. By engaging in dramatic play or structured role-playing activities, young people can explore different emotional scenarios and practice responding to various social situations. For example, in a classroom setting, students might participate in a role-playing exercise where they act out a conflict between friends. Through this process, they learn to recognize the emotions of others, consider multiple viewpoints, and explore potential resolutions. These experiences help children and adolescents develop emotional sensitivity and the ability to navigate complex social dynamics.

Beyond empathy, role-playing also plays a key role in the development of social skills. Successful social interactions require individuals to interpret social cues, manage their own emotions, and communicate effectively. Role-playing provides a safe space for practicing these skills, allowing individuals to experiment with different approaches to social situations without the fear of real-world consequences. For instance, in a role-playing scenario where participants must negotiate a solution to a problem, they practice essential skills such as active listening, collaboration, and compromise. These skills are critical for maintaining healthy interpersonal relationships and functioning effectively in group settings.

One of the unique advantages of role-playing in developing social skills is that it allows individuals to experience both sides of a social interaction. In a structured role-playing exercise, participants might switch roles to see the situation from multiple perspectives. For example, one participant might play the role of a person asking for help, while the other plays the role of the helper. By experiencing both perspectives, participants gain a deeper understanding of the social dynamics involved and develop a more nuanced approach to social interaction. This kind of experiential learning is particularly effective for individuals who struggle with social communication, such as those with autism spectrum disorder (ASD) or social anxiety.

Role-playing is also used in therapeutic settings to help individuals develop social skills and manage social anxiety. Cognitive-behavioral therapy (CBT) often incorporates role-playing exercises to help individuals practice social interactions in a controlled and supportive environment. For example, a therapist might guide a client through a role-playing scenario where they practice initiating a conversation or resolving a conflict. These exercises help individuals build confidence in their social abilities, reduce anxiety in social situations, and develop a toolkit of strategies for managing real-life social challenges.

How Storytelling Shapes Critical Thinking

Storytelling is a fundamental aspect of human communication, allowing individuals to share experiences, convey information, and explore complex ideas. In the context of drama and role-playing, storytelling serves as a powerful tool for shaping critical thinking and problem-solving skills. When individuals engage in storytelling, whether through improvisation, scripted drama, or narrative role-playing, they are required to construct coherent and meaningful narratives that make sense of the events and actions within the story. This process of organizing and interpreting information fosters critical thinking, as individuals must evaluate the logic of their story, anticipate potential outcomes, and consider the motivations of their characters.

One of the ways that storytelling promotes critical thinking is by encouraging participants to think about cause and effect relationships. In a narrative, every action has consequences, and participants must consider how the decisions made by their characters will impact the unfolding of the story. For example, in a role-playing scenario where participants are solving a mystery, they must carefully analyze the clues, make logical deductions, and predict the outcomes of their choices. This process mirrors real-life problem-solving, where individuals must evaluate different courses of action and consider the potential consequences of their decisions.

Storytelling also enhances analytical thinking by requiring individuals to break down complex scenarios into their component parts. When participants are crafting a story or playing a role, they must consider multiple factors, such as the motivations of the characters, the setting of the story, and the potential conflicts that may arise. This analytical process helps individuals develop the ability to think critically about complex situations, identify key elements, and draw connections between different aspects of the narrative. These skills are transferable to other areas of life, such as academic learning, where analytical thinking is essential for understanding complex concepts and solving problems.

Moreover, storytelling encourages divergent thinking, which is the ability to generate multiple possible solutions to a problem. In the context of drama and role-playing, participants are often required to improvise and think on their feet, creating new scenarios or adapting their characters' actions based on the evolving story. This process of improvisation fosters creativity and flexibility in thinking, as participants must explore different possibilities and consider alternative approaches to a situation. For example, in a role-playing game where participants must navigate a dangerous situation, they might come up with several potential solutions, such as negotiating with an adversary, using stealth to avoid conflict, or seeking help from an ally. This kind of creative problem-solving is essential for developing cognitive flexibility and adaptability.

In educational settings, storytelling and role-playing can be used to enhance critical thinking and engagement with complex topics. For example, students might participate in a role-playing activity where they reenact a historical event or debate a moral dilemma. Through this process, they are required to think critically about the issues involved, consider multiple perspectives, and evaluate the ethical implications of different actions. This type of experiential learning promotes deeper understanding and retention of the material, as students are actively engaged in the process of constructing knowledge rather than passively receiving information.

Storytelling also plays a key role in moral reasoning and the development of ethical decision-making. By engaging in narratives that involve moral dilemmas or conflicts, participants are encouraged to think critically about the values and principles that guide their actions. For example, in a role-playing scenario where a character must decide whether to lie to protect a friend, participants must weigh the consequences of honesty versus loyalty and consider the broader ethical implications of their choices. This process of moral reasoning helps individuals develop a more sophisticated understanding of ethical principles and strengthens their ability to navigate complex moral situations in real life.

Furthermore, storytelling and role-playing promote metacognition, or the ability to think about one's own thinking processes. As participants reflect on the actions and decisions of their characters, they gain insight into their own cognitive strategies and thought patterns. For example, after completing a role-playing exercise, participants might discuss what they learned about how they approach problem-solving, what strategies worked, and what they could improve. This kind of reflective thinking helps individuals develop self-awareness and improve their cognitive abilities over time.

Dramatic Play and Emotional Intelligence

Dramatic play, which involves imaginative role-playing and the enactment of scenarios, is a crucial component of emotional development, particularly in early childhood. Through dramatic play, children explore their emotions, practice emotional regulation, and develop a deeper understanding of their own feelings and the feelings of others. This form of play fosters emotional intelligence, which is the ability to recognize, understand, and manage emotions, as well as to navigate social relationships effectively.

One of the key ways that dramatic play enhances emotional intelligence is by providing a safe and supportive environment for emotional expression. Children often use dramatic play as a way to process their emotions and make sense of their experiences. For example, a child who is feeling anxious about starting school might enact a role-playing scenario where they pretend to be a teacher or student. Through this process, the child can explore their feelings of anxiety in a controlled and imaginative way, gaining a sense of mastery over the situation. This kind of emotional exploration is essential for helping children develop emotional resilience and the ability to cope with challenging situations.

Dramatic play also encourages emotional regulation, as children learn to manage their emotions in response to different scenarios. For example, in a role-playing game where a child takes on the role of a doctor, they must remain calm and composed while caring for a patient, even if the scenario is stressful or challenging. This process of staying in character helps children practice controlling their emotions and responding to situations in a thoughtful and measured way. Over time, these skills translate into real-life emotional regulation, as children become more adept at managing their feelings in a variety of situations.

Another important aspect of dramatic play is its role in fostering empathy and perspective-taking. When children engage in role-playing, they must consider the thoughts and feelings of the characters they are portraying, which helps them develop a deeper understanding of others' emotions and perspectives. For instance, in a scenario where a child plays the role of a caregiver or a friend, they must empathize with the character they are interacting with, imagining how that person might feel in different situations. This practice of stepping into anther's emotional shoes helps children refine their ability to understand and respond to the feelings of others, which is a critical component of emotional intelligence.

Empathy and emotional intelligence developed through dramatic play extend beyond early childhood and into later stages of life. In adolescence and adulthood, role-playing and drama-based activities continue to offer valuable opportunities for refining emotional understanding and regulation. Drama classes, improvisational theater, and therapeutic role-playing scenarios provide structured environments where individuals can explore complex emotions and learn to express them in healthy ways. The process of acting out different roles allows individuals to experiment with various emotional responses and learn how to manage their own emotions more effectively in real-life situations.

In therapeutic settings, drama therapy has been used to help individuals process trauma, explore unresolved emotional conflicts, and develop healthier emotional regulation strategies. Drama therapy allows individuals to externalize their emotions through role-playing, giving them the opportunity to safely explore difficult feelings and experiences. For example, a person who has experienced trauma might engage in a role-playing exercise where they act out a confrontation with their trauma in a safe and supportive environment. This process helps them gain insight into their emotional responses and develop new coping mechanisms for managing their feelings in the real world.

Social-emotional learning (SEL) programs, which are increasingly integrated into schools, also incorporate elements of dramatic play and role-playing to help children and adolescents develop emotional intelligence. These programs use role-playing scenarios to teach students how to recognize and regulate their emotions, empathize with others, and navigate social interactions effectively. By participating in these activities, students practice key emotional skills, such as identifying different emotions, understanding how emotions influence behavior, and using strategies to manage difficult emotions.

One of the key benefits of dramatic play in the development of emotional intelligence is that it allows individuals to experiment with different emotional responses and learn from the outcomes of their actions. For example, in a role-playing scenario where a child acts out a conflict with a peer, they might experiment with different ways of responding to the conflict, such as expressing their frustration calmly or escalating the situation with anger. Through this process, they learn which emotional responses lead to positive outcomes and which ones may worsen the situation. This type of experiential learning helps individuals develop greater emotional awareness and control, as they become more mindful of how their emotions influence their actions and relationships.

Dramatic play also fosters the development of self-awareness, which is the ability to recognize and understand one's own emotions. When individuals engage in role-playing, they are often encouraged to reflect on how their character feels and why they are behaving in a certain way. This process of introspection helps individuals become more attuned to their own emotional states and the factors that influence their behavior. Over time, this self-awareness contributes to better emotional regulation, as individuals learn to identify their emotional triggers and use appropriate strategies to manage their emotions.

In addition to self-awareness, dramatic play enhances relationship skills by providing individuals with the opportunity to practice social interactions in a safe and controlled environment. For example, in a role-playing scenario where two participants act out a negotiation or conflict resolution, they must practice effective communication, active listening, and cooperation. These skills are essential for building healthy relationships, as they enable individuals to navigate social interactions with empathy and understanding. By practicing these skills through dramatic play, individuals become more confident in their ability to handle real-life social situations, leading to stronger and more positive relationships.

Cognitive empathy, the ability to understand another person's perspective, is another key element of emotional intelligence that is developed through dramatic play. When individuals engage in role-playing, they are not only practicing emotional empathy (the ability to feel what another person is feeling) but also cognitive empathy, which involves understanding the thoughts, beliefs, and motivations of others. This process of cognitive perspective-taking is essential for navigating complex social interactions, as it helps individuals anticipate how others might think and feel in different situations.

For example, in a role-playing scenario where participants act out a court-room drama, they must consider the perspectives of multiple characters, such as the defense attorney, the prosecutor, and the judge. By taking on these different roles, participants practice thinking from various viewpoints, which enhances their ability to understand the thoughts and motivations of others in real-life situations. This skill is particularly valuable in professional settings, where individuals must often navigate conflicting perspectives and find common ground in order to achieve collaborative goals.

Moreover, dramatic play encourages individuals to explore emotional resilience, which is the ability to recover from emotional setbacks and adapt to challenging situations. In dramatic scenarios, participants often face emotionally charged situations, such as conflict, loss, or failure. By acting out these scenarios in a safe and supportive environment, individuals learn how to manage their emotional responses and recover from difficult experiences. This practice of emotional resilience helps individuals develop the skills they need to cope with real-life challenges and maintain their emotional well-being in the face of adversity.

Dramatic play also plays a role in the development of emotional expression. In many cases, individuals may struggle to express their emotions verbally or may feel uncomfortable sharing their feelings in direct conversations. Role-playing provides an alternative way to express emotions, as individuals can use their characters to explore and communicate their feelings in a less direct and potentially less threatening manner. For example, a child who is feeling angry or frustrated might act out those emotions through a character in a dramatic play scenario, allowing them to express their feelings without directly confronting the source of their frustration. This process of indirect emotional expression helps individuals process their emotions in a healthy and constructive way.

Finally, dramatic play fosters collaborative problem-solving and teamwork. Many role-playing activities involve working with others to achieve a common goal or resolve a conflict. This collaborative aspect of dramatic play encourages individuals to practice important social skills, such as negotiation, cooperation, and conflict resolution. By working together in a role-playing scenario, participants learn how to communicate effectively, listen to others' perspectives, and find solutions that benefit the group as a whole. These skills are essential for success in both personal and professional relationships, as they enable individuals to navigate complex social dynamics and work collaboratively toward shared goals.

In conclusion, drama and role-playing offer a powerful and multifaceted approach to cognitive and emotional development. By enhancing empathy, refining social skills, and promoting emotional intelligence, dramatic play helps individuals develop the skills they need to navigate the complexities of social interactions and manage their emotions effectively. Storytelling and role-playing also play a critical role in shaping critical thinking and problem-solving abilities, as participants are required to construct and evaluate narratives, analyze cause-and-effect relationships, and consider multiple perspectives. Through these processes, drama and role-playing provide individuals with the tools they need to succeed in both their personal and professional lives, fostering a deeper understanding of themselves and others.

Creative Writing: Fostering Imagination and Cognitive Skills

C reative writing is more than just a form of artistic expression; it is a powerful tool for fostering imagination and developing cognitive skills. Through the process of crafting stories, individuals engage in activities that stimulate various areas of the brain responsible for problem-solving, memory, analytical thinking, communication, and language development. By exploring the ways in which creative writing promotes cognitive growth, we can better understand its significance in both educational settings and personal development. Writing offers individuals the opportunity to think critically, express themselves creatively, and enhance their overall cognitive abilities.

The Power of Storytelling for Problem-Solving

Storytelling is an ancient form of communication that has shaped human culture for centuries. In the context of creative writing, storytelling serves as a means of exploring complex ideas, constructing narratives, and solving problems. The process of creating a story requires writers to think critically about cause-and-effect relationships, anticipate outcomes, and develop coherent solutions to narrative challenges. This makes storytelling an ideal medium for practicing and enhancing problem-solving skills.

One of the key cognitive processes involved in storytelling is narrative construction, which requires writers to organize events in a logical and meaningful way. When individuals create stories, they must decide how the plot will unfold, what conflicts will arise, and how those conflicts will be resolved. This process mirrors real-life problem-solving, where individuals are required to evaluate different options, anticipate potential consequences, and make decisions that lead to the desired outcome. For example, when a writer constructs a story about a character facing a difficult decision, they must consider the possible consequences of each choice the character might make and determine how those choices will impact the resolution of the story. This kind of thinking helps writers develop strategic planning and decision-making skills, which are essential for problem-solving in both personal and professional contexts.

Moreover, creative writing encourages divergent thinking, which is the ability to generate multiple possible solutions to a problem. In storytelling, writers are often faced with the challenge of creating original and compelling narratives that engage readers. To do this, they must think creatively and explore a variety of potential plot developments, character motivations, and resolutions. This process of generating multiple ideas and exploring different possibilities fosters cognitive flexibility, which is a critical component of problem-solving. Cognitive flexibility allows individuals to adapt to new situations, consider alternative perspectives, and find innovative solutions to complex problems.

For example, in a story where a character is trying to escape from a dangerous situation, the writer must come up with several potential escape routes or strategies that the character could use. The writer might consider different options, such as using stealth, seeking help from an ally, or outsmarting the antagonist. This process of exploring multiple possibilities helps writers develop the ability to think on their feet and adapt their problem-solving strategies based on the evolving circumstances of the narrative.

In addition to fostering cognitive flexibility, creative writing also enhances logical reasoning and analytical thinking. Writers must ensure that the events of their stories follow a logical progression and that the characters' actions and motivations make sense within the context of the narrative. This requires careful planning and attention to detail, as writers must constantly evaluate whether the story elements are consistent and coherent. For example, if a character in a story suddenly changes their behavior without a clear explanation, the writer must find a way to justify this shift in behavior, either by providing additional background information or by developing a logical sequence of events that lead to the change.

This process of evaluating and refining the narrative helps writers develop their analytical skills, as they learn to identify inconsistencies, gaps in logic, and areas where the story could be improved. By practicing these skills in the context of creative writing, individuals become more adept at analyzing and solving problems in other areas of life, whether in academic, professional, or personal settings.

Storytelling also promotes emotional problem-solving, as it often involves exploring the inner lives of characters and the emotional challenges they face. In many stories, characters must navigate difficult emotional situations, such as conflicts with others, personal dilemmas, or feelings of loss or fear. As writers create these scenarios, they are required to think about how the characters will respond to their emotions and how those emotional responses will impact the resolution of the story. This process of emotional exploration helps writers develop a deeper understanding of human emotions and the ways in which emotions influence decision-making and problem-solving.

For example, in a story where a character is struggling with grief, the writer might explore how the character's emotions impact their ability to make decisions, interact with others, and ultimately overcome their loss. This kind of emotional problem-solving is essential for developing emotional intelligence, which is the ability to recognize, understand, and manage one's own emotions as well as the emotions of others. By practicing emotional problem-solving through storytelling, writers develop greater empathy and emotional awareness, which are critical skills for navigating complex social and emotional situations in real life.

Enhancing Communication and Language Skills Through Writing

Creative writing is one of the most effective ways to develop communication and language skills. The process of writing requires individuals to think carefully about word choice, sentence structure, and the overall clarity of their message. Whether writing fiction or non-fiction, writers must communicate their ideas in a way that is engaging, coherent, and understandable to their audience. This constant practice in crafting clear and compelling prose helps writers refine their language skills and become more effective communicators.

One of the primary ways that creative writing enhances language skills is by promoting a deeper understanding of syntax and grammar. As writers construct sentences, they must pay attention to the rules of language and ensure that their writing is grammatically correct. This process of editing and revising helps writers internalize the rules of language, making them more proficient in both written and verbal communication. Over time, this practice leads to greater fluency in language use, as writers become more comfortable manipulating sentence structures and experimenting with different forms of expression.

In addition to improving grammar and syntax, creative writing also enhances vocabulary development. Writers are constantly searching for the right words to convey their ideas, and this process of word selection encourages them to expand their vocabulary and experiment with new language. For example, when describing a character's emotions or setting the scene for a story, a writer might use a variety of descriptive words and phrases to create a vivid and engaging narrative. This practice of exploring different words and their meanings helps writers develop a richer and more nuanced understanding of language.

Creative writing also promotes narrative skills, which are essential for effective communication. Whether telling a personal story or writing a fictional narrative, writers must structure their ideas in a way that captures the reader's attention and conveys the intended message. This process of organizing and sequencing information helps writers develop their ability to tell coherent and engaging stories, both in writing and in conversation. Strong narrative skills are critical for effective communication in a variety of contexts, from personal relationships to professional presentations.

Moreover, creative writing encourages writers to consider the perspective of their audience, which is essential for clear and effective communication. When writing a story, writers must think about how their words will be interpreted by their readers and whether the message they are trying to convey is clear and understandable. This process of considering the audience's perspective helps writers develop empathy and communication strategies that are tailored to the needs and expectations of their audience. For example, when writing a story for young children, a writer might use simple language and short sentences to ensure that the story is accessible and engaging for their target audience. This ability to adapt communication styles based on the audience is a critical skill for effective communication in both personal and professional settings.

Another way that creative writing enhances communication skills is by promoting self-expression. Writing allows individuals to explore their thoughts, feelings, and experiences in a structured and deliberate way, helping them articulate their emotions and ideas more clearly. This process of self-expression is particularly important for individuals who may struggle with verbal communication, as it provides an alternative way to communicate their inner world. By practicing self-expression through writing, individuals develop greater confidence in their ability to communicate effectively and share their perspectives with others.

Creative writing also encourages individuals to engage with different forms of language and communication, such as dialogue, descriptive language, and metaphor. For example, when writing dialogue for characters, writers must think about how people speak in real life and how to convey personality, emotion, and intention through spoken language. This practice of writing dialogue helps writers develop their understanding of verbal communication and the ways in which tone, inflection, and word choice can convey meaning.

In addition to dialogue, creative writing often involves the use of figurative language, such as metaphors, similes, and symbolism, to convey deeper meaning and emotion. By experimenting with these forms of language, writers learn to communicate complex ideas and emotions in more subtle and nuanced ways. This ability to use figurative language enhances both written and verbal communication, as it allows individuals to convey meaning that goes beyond the literal interpretation of their words.

Overall, creative writing is a powerful tool for enhancing communication and language skills, as it provides individuals with the opportunity to practice and refine their ability to express themselves clearly, creatively, and effectively.

How Writing Stimulates Memory and Analytical Thinking

Writing is not only a creative process but also a cognitive exercise that engages memory, critical thinking, and analytical skills. When individuals write, they are required to retrieve information from memory, analyze that information, and organize it into a coherent structure. This process stimulates various areas of the brain responsible for memory consolidation, working memory, and analytical thinking, making writing an effective tool for cognitive development.

One of the key cognitive processes involved in writing is memory retrieval. Whether writing fiction or non-fiction, writers must draw on their knowledge, experiences, and memories to construct their narratives. For example, when writing a personal essay, an individual might recall specific events from their past, such as conversations, emotions, and sensory details. This process of recalling and organizing memories helps strengthen the neural connections involved in long-term memory and enhances the brain's ability to retrieve information effectively.

Writing also engages working memory, which refers to the brain's ability to hold and manipulate information for short periods while performing cognitive tasks. In creative writing, working memory is essential for keeping track of multiple elements of a story, such as character development, plot progression, and thematic coherence. For instance, when writing a novel, an author must remember details about each character's traits, motivations, and interactions while simultaneously crafting new scenes and dialogues. This juggling of information strengthens the capacity of working memory, enhancing overall cognitive function.

Beyond memory retrieval, writing also stimulates analytical thinking. The process of constructing a narrative requires writers to think critically about how different elements of a story fit together and whether the story follows a logical progression. Writers must continually evaluate their work, considering whether their characters' actions make sense, whether the plot flows smoothly, and whether the themes are conveyed effectively. This self-evaluation and refinement process sharpens analytical skills by requiring individuals to think deeply about structure, logic, and meaning.

In addition to analyzing their own work, writers often engage in comparative analysis by drawing inspiration from other literary works, genres, or writing styles. For example, a writer working on a mystery novel might analyze how other mystery writers build suspense or reveal clues. This process of analyzing and comparing different writing techniques fosters metacognition, or the ability to think about one's own thinking processes. Meta cognition is a key component of analytical thinking, as it helps individuals become more aware of their cognitive strategies and how to apply them effectively in different contexts.

Creative writing also promotes deductive reasoning and inductive reasoning, both of which are essential for analytical thinking. Deductive reasoning involves starting with a general principle and applying it to specific situations, while inductive reasoning involves observing specific details and using them to form a general conclusion. In writing, deductive reasoning might be used when a writer constructs a story based on a predetermined theme or message, ensuring that all elements of the story support that central idea. Inductive reasoning, on the other hand, might be used when a writer develops a character's personality based on their behavior and interactions in the story. By practicing both forms of reasoning through writing, individuals enhance their ability to analyze information, draw conclusions, and solve problems.

Writing also encourages pattern recognition, which is a critical skill for analytical thinking. Whether crafting a poem, short story, or novel, writers often work with patterns, such as recurring themes, motifs, or symbols, to give their work coherence and depth. Recognizing and using these patterns helps writers create more meaningful and structured narratives. Moreover, the process of identifying patterns in writing translates to other areas of life, such as academic learning or problem-solving, where recognizing underlying patterns is essential for understanding complex information.

In addition to promoting analytical thinking, writing also enhances creative problem-solving by encouraging individuals to think outside the box and explore unconventional ideas. Writers are often faced with narrative challenges, such as how to resolve a conflict, develop a character arc, or maintain suspense throughout a story. To overcome these challenges, writers must experiment with different approaches, think creatively, and find innovative solutions. For example, in a story where a protagonist is trapped in a seemingly impossible situation, the writer might explore several potential solutions before finding the most effective and surprising resolution. This process of creative problem-solving fosters cognitive flexibility, as it requires individuals to adapt their thinking and consider multiple possibilities.

Moreover, writing encourages individuals to engage in reflective thinking, which involves reviewing and analyzing one's past experiences or thoughts. When individuals write about their personal experiences or explore complex emotions through creative writing, they engage in a process of introspection and reflection. This reflective thinking helps individuals make sense of their experiences, gain new insights, and develop a deeper understanding of themselves and the world around them. For example, when writing a memoir or personal essay, a writer might reflect on how a particular life event shaped their beliefs, values, or relationships. This process of reflection not only strengthens memory but also enhances self-awareness and emotional intelligence.

Reflective thinking in writing also promotes cognitive resilience, which is the ability to adapt and recover from cognitive challenges or setbacks. Writing often involves multiple drafts, revisions, and edits, as writers work to refine their ideas and improve the quality of their work. This iterative process of trial and error fosters perseverance and resilience, as writers learn to overcome challenges and persist in the face of difficulties. The skills developed through this process—such as adaptability, persistence, and problem-solving—are essential for cognitive growth and success in various areas of life.

Another important cognitive benefit of writing is its ability to enhance abstract thinking. In creative writing, abstract thinking is required to explore complex themes, ideas, and emotions in ways that go beyond concrete or literal descriptions. For example, a writer might use symbolism, metaphor, or allegory to convey abstract concepts such as love, freedom, or justice. This ability to think abstractly is essential for understanding complex concepts in literature, philosophy, and science, as it allows individuals to grasp ideas that are not directly observable or measurable.

For example, in a dystopian novel, a writer might use a futuristic society as a metaphor for current social or political issues, encouraging readers to think critically about the implications of the story. This kind of abstract thinking enhances cognitive flexibility and analytical reasoning, as it requires individuals to make connections between seemingly unrelated ideas and explore the deeper meaning behind the narrative.

Writing also stimulates creative imagination, which is a critical aspect of cognitive development. Through the process of writing, individuals are encouraged to invent new worlds, characters, and scenarios that push the boundaries of reality. This exercise in imagination engages the default mode network (DMN) of the brain, which is responsible for daydreaming, creativity, and spontaneous thought. By engaging the DMN, writing encourages individuals to explore new ideas, envision alternative possibilities, and generate innovative solutions to problems. This creative engagement not only enhances imagination but also fosters a greater capacity for innovation and original thinking.

Creative writing also strengthens emotional memory, as it allows individuals to recall and process past emotional experiences. When writers explore the emotional lives of their characters or draw on their own emotions to enhance their stories, they engage the brain's limbic system, which is responsible for processing emotions and forming emotional memories. This emotional engagement helps writers develop a deeper understanding of their own emotions and the emotions of others, which enhances emotional intelligence and empathy.

In conclusion, creative writing serves as a powerful cognitive exercise that stimulates memory, enhances analytical thinking, and fosters imagination. Through the process of storytelling, individuals engage in problem-solving, develop communication and language skills, and practice both reflective and abstract thinking. Writing is not only a creative outlet but also a tool for cognitive growth, as it challenges individuals to think critically, explore new ideas, and refine their ability to communicate effectively. As such, creative writing plays a crucial role in fostering both intellectual and emotional development, making it an essential skill for success in personal, academic, and professional contexts.

The Impact of Arts Integration in Schools

Arts integration in schools has gained recognition as a powerful approach to enhancing cognitive development, creativity, and emotional well-being in students. By embedding arts into core academic subjects, schools can foster a richer, more engaging learning environment that nurtures multiple aspects of students' intellectual and personal growth. Research and case studies consistently demonstrate the cognitive and emotional benefits of arts-focused curricula, showing that students in art-rich learning environments often outperform their peers in both academic and non-academic areas. This chapter explores the impact of arts integration in schools, examining case studies, measuring cognitive growth, and identifying both challenges and opportunities in creating art-infused educational programs.

Case Studies of Schools with Art-Focused Curricula

Numerous schools around the world have embraced arts integration as a central component of their educational philosophy, with notable case studies demonstrating the trans-formative effects of art-rich curricula on students' cognitive development, academic performance, and emotional well-being. These case studies highlight how schools that prioritize arts education create environments where students not only thrive academically but also develop essential life skills such as problem-solving, critical thinking, and emotional resilience.

One prominent example is the Chicago Arts Partnership in Education (CAPE), which has been at the forefront of integrating the arts into core subjects like math, science, and language arts. CAPE collaborates with public schools to design interdisciplinary lessons that combine artistic practices with academic content. For instance, students learning about fractions in math might use visual arts to create representations of fractional parts, or they might compose songs that help them remember mathematical concepts. This blending of artistic expression with traditional academics has been shown to deepen students' understanding of the material, making abstract concepts more tangible and memorable.

In evaluations of CAPE schools, students consistently demonstrated higher levels of engagement, creativity, and academic achievement compared to their peers in non-arts-integrated schools. Teachers also reported that students developed stronger critical thinking skills and were more willing to take intellectual risks, as the arts provided a platform for exploration and experimentation without the fear of failure. Additionally, students in CAPE schools exhibited improved collaboration and communication skills, as many of the arts-integrated projects required them to work in teams and express their ideas through various artistic mediums.

Another successful case study is The Lincoln Center Education (LCE) program in New York City, which emphasizes aesthetic education as a means of fostering deep cognitive and emotional engagement. The program introduces students to professional works of art—whether through visual arts, dance, music, or theater—and then encourages them to reflect on and create their own responses to these works. The LCE model promotes inquiry-based learning, where students ask questions about the artistic process, explore different perspectives, and draw connections between the arts and other academic subjects.

One notable outcome of the LCE program is its ability to cultivate meta cognitive skills in students. By reflecting on their creative processes and analyzing the artistic choices they make, students develop a greater awareness of their own thinking and learning strategies. This kind of self-reflection is essential for cognitive growth, as it helps students become more intentional and thoughtful learners. Furthermore, LCE schools have reported improvements in students' emotional intelligence and empathy, as the arts encourage them to explore diverse cultural experiences and express their emotions in constructive ways.

In the United Kingdom, Creative Partnerships was a national program that brought together artists, educators, and cultural organizations to integrate the arts into school curricula. The program focused on using creative approaches to teaching and learning, particularly in under performing schools. Creative Partnerships aimed to engage students who were disengaged from traditional forms of education by offering them new ways to connect with academic content through the arts.

Studies on the impact of Creative Partnerships found that students in participating schools demonstrated significant improvements in academic performance, particularly in literacy and numeracy. The creative methods used in these schools helped students develop a deeper understanding of complex subjects and provided alternative ways for them to express their knowledge. For example, students learning about historical events might create a theatrical performance that brings those events to life, allowing them to explore historical perspectives in a more dynamic and immersive way. Creative Partnerships also helped foster a positive school culture, where students were more motivated to learn and take pride in their creative achievements.

Measuring Cognitive Growth in Art-Rich Learning Environments

One of the central challenges in evaluating the impact of arts integration in schools is finding effective ways to measure cognitive growth in students. Traditional standardized testing, which focuses on memorization and rote learning, may not fully capture the intellectual and emotional benefits of arts integration. However, researchers have developed various methods to assess the cognitive and developmental outcomes of students in art-rich learning environments, demonstrating that these programs contribute to significant cognitive gains.

Executive function, a set of cognitive processes that includes working memory, cognitive flexibility, and inhibitory control, has been shown to improve in students who engage in arts-integrated learning. These cognitive functions are essential for problem-solving, decision-making, and adapting to new situations—all skills that are reinforced through artistic activities. For example, when students participate in theater or dance performances, they must remember choreography or lines, adapt to the dynamics of a live performance, and regulate their emotions in front of an audience. These activities engage the prefrontal cortex, which is responsible for executive function, and help strengthen neural connections related to cognitive control.

Research by James S. Catterall and his colleagues has provided compelling evidence of the positive effects of arts integration on cognitive development. Catterall's study, "The Arts and Achievement in At-Risk Youth," examined the long-term effects of arts participation on academic performance, social behavior, and cognitive outcomes. The study found that students who were consistently involved in the arts outperformed their peers in standardized tests, demonstrated higher levels of motivation, and were more likely to pursue higher education. Additionally, the study revealed that arts participation helped students develop a greater sense of agency and self-efficacy, which contributed to improved academic and personal outcomes.

Creative thinking is another area where cognitive growth can be measured in art-rich learning environments. Creative thinking involves the ability to generate novel ideas, make connections between seemingly unrelated concepts, and approach problems from multiple perspectives. Arts integration fosters this kind of thinking by encouraging students to explore different mediums of expression, experiment with new ideas, and take creative risks. Measuring creative thinking often involves assessments such as the Torrance Tests of Creative Thinking (TTCT), which evaluate fluency, originality, and flexibility in students' responses to open-ended prompts. Studies using the TTCT have shown that students in arts-integrated programs score higher in creative thinking abilities compared to those in traditional learning environments.

Additionally, arts integration has been linked to improvements in spatial reasoning, which is the ability to understand and manipulate objects in space. Spatial reasoning is a critical cognitive skill for success in subjects such as mathematics, science, and engineering. Research has shown that students who engage in visual arts, such as drawing, sculpture, or architecture, develop stronger spatial reasoning skills because these activities require them to think about proportion, perspective, and the relationships between objects. For example, a student who creates a three-dimensional model of a building must consider the spatial arrangement of the structure, which helps develop their ability to visualize and manipulate spatial information.

Another key aspect of cognitive growth in art-rich learning environments is the development of emotional intelligence, which refers to the ability to recognize, understand, and manage emotions. Emotional intelligence is closely linked to cognitive processes such as decision-making, conflict resolution, and interpersonal communication. Arts integration provides students with opportunities to express their emotions through creative mediums, such as music, theater, or visual arts, which helps them develop greater emotional awareness and regulation. This emotional engagement enhances students' ability to navigate social situations and make informed decisions, both in school and in their personal lives.

Challenges and Opportunities in Integrating Arts

While the benefits of arts integration in schools are well-documented, there are also significant challenges associated with implementing and sustaining these programs. One of the primary challenges is funding. Many schools, particularly those in undeserved communities, struggle to secure the financial resources needed to support arts education. Budget constraints often lead to cuts in arts programs, as schools prioritize subjects like math and reading, which are more directly tied to standardized testing outcomes. This lack of funding can limit students' access to quality arts education, especially in public schools that already face financial difficulties.

To overcome this challenge, some schools have sought partnerships with local arts organizations, museums, and cultural institutions. These partnerships provide schools with access to additional resources, such as professional artists, art supplies, and performance spaces, at little or no cost. For example, CAPE collaborates with local artists and organizations to bring creative professionals into classrooms, offering students opportunities to work with experts in various artistic disciplines. These partnerships also help build a bridge between schools and the broader community, creating a more inclusive and supportive environment for arts education.

Another challenge in integrating the arts is the lack of professional development opportunities for teachers. Many educators may not feel confident in their ability to teach or incorporate the arts into their lessons, particularly if they have little experience or training in artistic disciplines. Providing professional development for teachers is essential for the successful implementation of arts integration, as it equips educators with the tools and strategies they need to design effective, interdisciplinary lessons. Some schools and districts have addressed this challenge by offering workshops, seminars, and coaching programs for teachers, where they can learn how to use the arts to enhance their instruction in core academic subjects.

The standardized testing culture in many school systems also poses a challenge to arts integration. Schools are often under pressure to meet specific performance targets on standardized tests, which can lead to a narrow focus on testable subjects like math and reading. This emphasis on standardized testing may leave little room for creative exploration or arts-based learning, as teachers feel compelled to "teach to the test." However, proponents of arts integration argue that the arts can actually improve performance in tested subjects by making learning more engaging and accessible. By shifting the focus from memorization to deeper cognitive engagement, arts-integrated lessons help students develop critical thinking, problem-solving, and analytical skills, which can enhance their performance in traditional academic subjects as well. Schools that have successfully integrated arts into their curriculum often see improvements in test scores and academic achievement, challenging the assumption that arts education detracts from core academic learning.

Another challenge is the lack of time in the school day to implement arts-integrated lessons. Teachers are often constrained by tight schedules that prioritize covering academic content, leaving little room for creative exploration or interdisciplinary activities. Finding time to incorporate arts-based learning requires a shift in how schools allocate time and resources. Some schools have addressed this issue by incorporating arts integration into existing subjects rather than treating the arts as a separate class. For example, a science lesson might include a visual arts component, such as having students draw diagrams or models to explain scientific concepts, or a history lesson might involve students performing a dramatic reenactment of historical events.

Despite these challenges, there are also numerous opportunities for integrating the arts into schools, particularly as educators and policymakers recognize the broader cognitive and emotional benefits of arts education. One significant opportunity is the growing support for social-emotional learning (SEL), which focuses on helping students develop emotional intelligence, empathy, and interpersonal skills. The arts, particularly theater, music, and visual arts, provide a natural platform for SEL, as they encourage students to explore their emotions, collaborate with others, and express themselves in constructive ways. Integrating the arts into SEL programs can help students build the emotional resilience and social skills they need to succeed both in school and in life.

There is also increasing recognition of the role that the arts can play in promoting equity and inclusion in education. Art has the power to break down barriers and provide a voice for students from diverse backgrounds, including those who may feel marginalized in traditional academic settings. By integrating the arts into the curriculum, schools can create more inclusive learning environments that celebrate diversity and encourage students to share their unique cultural perspectives. For example, schools might integrate cultural art forms into lessons, such as incorporating African drumming into a music class or exploring Indigenous storytelling traditions in a language arts lesson. This approach not only fosters cultural understanding but also provides students with opportunities to see their identities and experiences reflected in the curriculum.

Moreover, the rise of digital and media arts presents new opportunities for arts integration in schools. As technology continues to play an increasingly central role in education, many schools are exploring how digital arts—such as film production, animation, graphic design, and photography—can be incorporated into the curriculum. Digital arts offer students new ways to engage with academic content, express their creativity, and develop technical skills that are highly relevant in today's workforce. For example, students might create short films to illustrate historical events or use graphic design software to design posters for a science project. These digital arts projects not only enhance students' creative and technical skills but also deepen their understanding of core academic subjects.

The potential for arts integration to foster cross-curricular connections is another key opportunity. When the arts are integrated into subjects like math, science, and language arts, students are encouraged to make connections between different areas of knowledge, leading to a more holistic understanding of the world. For instance, a project that combines math and visual arts might involve students using geometric shapes to create art, helping them develop both mathematical reasoning and artistic creativity. Similarly, a music project might explore the physics of sound, allowing students to apply scientific concepts to a creative endeavor. These interdisciplinary connections help students see how different subjects are interconnected and encourage them to think critically about how knowledge in one domain can inform understanding in another.

Finally, the increasing focus on 21st-century skills, such as creativity, collaboration, communication, and critical thinking, presents a significant opportunity for expanding arts integration in schools. As the workforce continues to evolve, with an emphasis on innovation and adaptability, there is growing recognition that students need more than just traditional academic skills to succeed. The arts, with their emphasis on creative problem-solving, teamwork, and self-expression, are uniquely positioned to help students develop the skills they need to thrive in a rapidly changing world. Schools that embrace arts integration can help students cultivate these 21st-century skills while also enhancing their cognitive, emotional, and social development.

In conclusion, while there are challenges to integrating the arts into schools, such as funding, time constraints, and the pressure of standardized testing, the opportunities far outweigh these obstacles. Arts integration offers a powerful way to enhance cognitive growth, foster creativity, and promote emotional well-being in students. By embedding the arts into academic subjects, schools can create rich, engaging learning environments that not only improve academic performance but also nurture the whole child—developing their intellect, creativity, and emotional resilience. Schools that successfully integrate the arts into their curricula provide students with the tools they need to become innovative thinkers, empathetic leaders, and lifelong learners, prepared to face the challenges and opportunities of the future.

Creative Arts for All Ages: From Early Childhood to Adolescence

C reative arts play a significant role in fostering cognitive, emotional, and social development at every stage of life. From early childhood to adolescence, engaging in artistic activities enhances various aspects of cognitive growth and provides individuals with tools for self-expression, problem-solving, and emotional regulation. The creative arts offer a unique and flexible way to support brain development and stimulate learning in ways that traditional academic activities may not fully capture. By tailoring creative activities to the specific developmental needs of each age group, educators and caregivers can maximize the impact of the arts on cognitive growth and emotional resilience.

Cognitive Growth Stages and Appropriate Artistic Activities

The cognitive development of children unfolds in distinct stages, each marked by specific changes in brain structure and function. According to developmental theorists such as Jean Piaget, these stages reflect the progressive nature of learning, where children move from sensory exploration to abstract reasoning. Throughout these stages, engaging in creative arts can facilitate key cognitive functions and contribute to overall mental development.

Early childhood (ages 0-5) is marked by rapid brain growth, where children begin to explore the world through their senses and motor skills. At this stage, artistic activities that emphasize sensory experience and fine motor coordination are essential for fostering cognitive development. Activities such as finger painting, scribbling, playing with clay, or manipulating objects like blocks and beads allow young children to explore textures, shapes, and colors while developing their sensorimotor skills. These early explorations not only help children develop control over their body movements but also encourage visual-spatial processing, which is critical for later problem-solving and reasoning skills.

Additionally, the arts provide an avenue for symbolic thinking—the ability to represent objects and experiences through symbols—which is a foundational cognitive skill that emerges in early childhood. For example, when a child draws a stick figure to represent a person or uses a block to symbolize a car, they are engaging in symbolic thinking. This ability to think symbolically is a precursor to more advanced cognitive tasks such as reading, writing, and mathematical reasoning. Creative arts activities that involve pretend play, such as using puppets, costumes, or props, further promote symbolic thinking and help children make sense of the world around them.

As children transition into middle childhood (ages 6-11), their cognitive abilities become more sophisticated. At this stage, children are better able to engage in logical reasoning, cause-and-effect thinking, and more complex problem-solving tasks. Artistic activities that challenge children to think critically and creatively are especially beneficial during this period. For example, drawing, painting, and sculpture can be used to introduce children to concepts like symmetry, proportion, and perspective, which require them to apply their reasoning skills to create balanced and visually coherent works of art. These activities also enhance fine motor skills and hand-eye coordination, as children learn to manipulate tools such as brushes, pencils, and scissors with greater precision.

Creative activities that involve storytelling, such as writing poems or creating comic strips, also promote cognitive growth by encouraging children to organize their thoughts, structure narratives, and express ideas through language and imagery. These activities help improve language skills and working memory, as children must remember details about their characters and plot while creating their stories. In addition, engaging in collaborative art projects, such as group murals or theater performances, fosters social cognition, as children learn to cooperate, share ideas, and navigate group dynamics.

During adolescence (ages 12-18), the brain undergoes significant changes, particularly in areas related to executive function, emotional regulation, and abstract reasoning. The prefrontal cortex, which is responsible for planning, decision-making, and impulse control, continues to develop during this stage. Artistic activities that encourage abstract thinking and emotional exploration are particularly valuable for adolescents, as they provide opportunities for self-expression and introspection. For example, engaging in abstract painting, creative writing, or theatrical performance allows adolescents to explore complex emotions and ideas that may be difficult to articulate verbally.

Artistic activities can also promote critical thinking and metacognition—the ability to think about one's own thinking processes. When adolescents create art, they are often required to reflect on their creative choices, analyze their work, and make adjustments to improve the final product. This process of self-reflection helps adolescents develop greater awareness of their own cognitive strategies and decision-making processes, which is essential for academic and personal success.

Tailoring Creative Activities to Different Age Groups

While the creative arts offer benefits for individuals of all ages, it is important to tailor artistic activities to the specific developmental needs of each age group. By doing so, educators and caregivers can ensure that the activities are both cognitively stimulating and developmentally appropriate.

In early childhood, artistic activities should focus on sensory exploration and the development of basic motor skills. At this stage, children are naturally curious and eager to explore their environment through touch, sight, and movement. Activities such as finger painting, playing with modeling clay, or engaging in rhythmic dance allow young children to experiment with textures, colors, and sounds while developing their sensory awareness and coordination. These activities are not only enjoyable but also help children develop the fine motor skills they will need for tasks such as writing, drawing, and using tools later in life.

Artistic activities for this age group should also encourage imaginative play, which is critical for the development of symbolic thinking and social skills. For example, children might engage in pretend play by using costumes or props to act out stories, or they might create simple drawings that represent their favorite animals or family members. These activities help children develop their ability to represent and organize information, laying the foundation for more complex cognitive tasks such as reading and problem-solving.

As children enter middle childhood, they become more capable of engaging in structured and goal-oriented artistic activities. At this stage, activities that challenge children to think critically and creatively are especially beneficial. For example, educators might introduce step-by-step drawing or sculpture projects that require children to follow instructions while also making their own creative choices. These activities help children develop their planning and organizational skills while encouraging them to experiment with different artistic techniques.

Creative writing is also an excellent activity for children in middle childhood, as it promotes language development, narrative skills, and empathy. By writing stories, poems, or plays, children practice organizing their thoughts, developing characters, and expressing their emotions through language. This type of activity also encourages children to put themselves in the shoes of their characters, fostering empathy and a deeper understanding of different perspectives.

For adolescents, artistic activities should provide opportunities for self-expression and critical thinking. Adolescence is a time of heightened emotional sensitivity and cognitive complexity, as individuals begin to explore their identities, values, and beliefs. Engaging in artistic activities that allow for introspection and emotional exploration can help adolescents process their emotions and develop a stronger sense of self.

Creative writing, such as journalism, poetry, or short story writing, is a valuable outlet for adolescents to express their thoughts and feelings. Writing allows them to explore complex ideas, work through personal challenges, and gain insight into their own emotional experiences. In addition to writing, visual arts such as drawing, painting, and photography provide adolescents with opportunities to express themselves through imagery, which can be particularly beneficial for those who may find it difficult to articulate their emotions verbally.

Performing arts, such as theater and dance, also offer adolescents a powerful way to explore their emotions and develop their social skills. Acting in plays or participating in dance performances requires adolescents to step into different roles, consider different perspectives, and work collaboratively with others. These activities not only enhance emotional intelligence but also help adolescents build confidence in their ability to communicate and connect with others.

How Adolescents Benefit from Creative Exploration

Adolescence is a critical period for creative exploration, as it coincides with significant cognitive, emotional, and social development. During this stage, individuals are beginning to form their identities, develop their worldviews, and explore their passions. Creative arts offer adolescents a unique and powerful way to navigate this complex developmental phase, providing them with opportunities for self-expression, emotional processing, and intellectual growth.

One of the key benefits of creative exploration during adolescence is the development of abstract thinking and higher-order reasoning. As the prefrontal cortex continues to mature, adolescents become more capable of thinking critically, evaluating multiple perspectives, and considering hypothetical scenarios. Artistic activities that encourage symbolic representation, metaphor, and abstract expression help adolescents refine these cognitive abilities. For example, creating a painting that represents an abstract concept like freedom or justice challenges adolescents to think metaphorically and communicate complex ideas through visual language.

Creative exploration also plays a significant role in fostering emotional intelligence in adolescents. Engaging in the arts allows them to explore their emotions in a safe and constructive way, helping them better understand and manage their feelings. For example, an adolescent who writes poetry might use the medium to process feelings of loneliness, frustration, or joy. By articulating these emotions through creative expression, adolescents can gain insight into their emotional states and develop healthier ways of coping with stress or difficult experiences.

In addition to emotional regulation, creative exploration helps adolescents build resilience and self-efficacy. The process of creating art—whether writing a story, composing a piece of music, or completing a painting—often involves overcoming challenges, such as dealing with creative blocks or experimenting with new techniques. By working through these challenges and ultimately producing a finished work, adolescents develop a sense of accomplishment and confidence in their ability to persevere and achieve their goals. This sense of self-efficacy extends beyond the arts and contributes to greater resilience in other areas of life, such as academics, relationships, and future career pursuits.

Creative exploration also provides adolescents with opportunities for social connection and collaboration. Participating in group art projects, theater productions, or music ensembles fosters a sense of community and teamwork among adolescents. In these settings, they learn how to collaborate with others, share ideas, and respect diverse perspectives. Group creative activities also help adolescents develop important social communication skills, as they must express their ideas clearly, listen to their peers, and work together to achieve a common goal. These collaborative experiences can be especially valuable for building friendships and developing interpersonal skills, both of which are critical during adolescence as social relationships become more central to their identity formation.

The arts also offer adolescents a space for identity exploration, which is a key task during this developmental stage. Adolescents often grapple with questions about who they are, where they fit in the world, and what they value. Creative activities, such as writing, painting, or acting, provide them with a platform to explore these questions and experiment with different aspects of their identity. For example, an adolescent might write a short story about a character facing a moral dilemma, using the narrative to explore their own beliefs and values. Similarly, participating in a theater production might allow an adolescent to experiment with different roles and personas, helping them gain a deeper understanding of themselves and how they relate to others.

Engaging in the arts can also serve as a cultural exploration tool for adolescents, offering them the opportunity to learn about and appreciate diverse cultures and artistic traditions. Through creative activities, adolescents can explore their own cultural heritage, as well as those of others, fostering a sense of global awareness and empathy. For example, studying the art forms of different cultures—such as African drumming, Japanese calligraphy, or Latin American dance—can broaden adolescents' perspectives and help them appreciate the richness of human expression across the world. This exposure to different cultural art forms encourages tolerance, empathy, and a deeper understanding of diversity, which are essential skills for navigating an increasingly interconnected world.

Creative arts also help adolescents develop self-discipline and time management skills. The process of creating a work of art, whether it's a painting, a piece of music, or a play, requires commitment, focus, and the ability to manage one's time effectively. For adolescents, learning to set goals, follow through on creative projects, and meet deadlines are valuable life skills that will serve them well in future academic and professional endeavors. For instance, an adolescent working on a year-end art portfolio or preparing for a school musical must practice self-regulation by setting aside time to rehearse, plan, and revise their work. These experiences teach adolescents the importance of perseverance and dedication, which are key components of success in any field.

Another benefit of creative exploration for adolescents is the development of critical thinking and problem-solving abilities. Artistic endeavors often require adolescents to think outside the box, experiment with new ideas, and find creative solutions to challenges. Whether they are figuring out how to portray a complex emotion in a painting or how to resolve a plot conflict in a story, adolescents must apply critical thinking skills to overcome obstacles in their creative work. This type of problem-solving fosters cognitive flexibility, allowing adolescents to approach challenges from multiple angles and devise innovative solutions.

Furthermore, creative risk-taking is an important aspect of adolescent development that the arts encourage. Adolescence is a time of experimentation and self-discovery, and engaging in creative arts gives adolescents a safe space to take risks, try new things, and push the boundaries of their creativity. Whether it's experimenting with a new artistic medium, performing in front of an audience for the first time, or sharing their personal writing with others, these experiences build confidence and encourage adolescents to step outside of their comfort zones. The ability to take creative risks helps adolescents develop a growth mindset, where they see challenges as opportunities for learning and growth rather than as threats to their self-esteem.

Finally, creative arts provide a powerful outlet for mental health and emotional well-being in adolescents. The teenage years are often marked by heightened emotions, social pressures, and identity struggles, which can lead to feelings of anxiety, stress, or depression. Engaging in creative activities allows adolescents to express their emotions in a healthy and constructive way, providing them with a sense of release and relief from the pressures they may be facing. For example, writing poetry or journalism can help adolescents process their emotions, while drawing or painting can serve as a form of meditation and self-reflection. These creative outlets can have a positive impact on adolescents' mental health, helping them develop coping mechanisms that promote emotional resilience.

In conclusion, the creative arts offer immense cognitive, emotional, and social benefits for individuals across all stages of development, from early childhood to adolescence. By tailoring artistic activities to the developmental needs of each age group, educators and caregivers can help children and adolescents maximize their cognitive growth, emotional regulation, and social skills. For adolescents in particular, creative exploration provides a platform for identity formation, emotional expression, and critical thinking, all of which are crucial for navigating the challenges of adolescence and preparing for adulthood. As such, integrating creative arts into the educational experiences of young people is essential for fostering their holistic development and supporting their lifelong success.

Art and Special Needs Education: Unlocking Potential

C reative arts offer powerful tools for unlocking potential and supporting cognitive, emotional, and social development in children with special needs. Art can provide alternative means of communication, allowing children with disabilities to express themselves in ways that verbal or traditional academic methods may not support. For children with physical, cognitive, or emotional challenges, engaging in creative arts offers a more flexible, sensory-driven approach to learning, one that can be tailored to individual needs and abilities. This chapter explores how creative arts support learning for children with special needs, examines adaptive art techniques that promote cognitive development, and highlights case studies of successful art-based interventions.

How Creative Arts Support Learning for Children with Special Needs

Children with special needs, including those with cognitive impairments, autism spectrum disorder (ASD), attention-deficit/hyperactivity disorder (ADHD), and physical disabilities, often require differentiated learning strategies to reach their full potential. Traditional education models may not always provide the most effective methods for these learners, which is where creative arts come into play. The arts offer a multi-sensory approach that engages multiple brain regions simultaneously, creating opportunities for growth in areas such as communication, motor skills, emotional regulation, and social interaction.

One of the most significant benefits of creative arts for children with special needs is the way they facilitate communication and expression. Many children with disabilities, particularly those with ASD or speech impairments, may struggle to express their thoughts, feelings, and needs through verbal communication. Creative arts—such as painting, drawing, sculpture, music, and dance—provide these children with non-verbal outlets for self-expression. For example, a child with limited verbal skills may use colors, shapes, or textures to represent their emotions or convey ideas they cannot articulate in words. This form of artistic expression not only provides a means of communication but also fosters a sense of accomplishment and self-worth as children see their ideas and feelings represented in tangible forms.

In addition to supporting communication, creative arts enhance cognitive development by promoting problem-solving, critical thinking, and sensory integration. For children with cognitive impairments, engaging in artistic activities can help strengthen neural pathways involved in executive function, spatial reasoning, and memory. Art projects often require children to plan, organize materials, and make decisions about colors, shapes, and composition. These tasks activate the prefrontal cortex, which is responsible for higher-order thinking, decision-making, and attention control. Through the creative process, children develop their ability to focus, organize their thoughts, and approach problems from multiple angles.

Another important aspect of creative arts is their role in improving fine and gross motor skills, which are essential for physical development. Many children with special needs, such as those with cerebral palsy or developmental coordination disorder (DCD), experience difficulties with motor control and coordination. Activities like drawing, painting, or working with clay require children to practice precise movements, enhancing their hand-eye coordination and fine motor skills. For children with physical disabilities, adaptive tools—such as modified brushes, grips, or touch-sensitive surfaces— can be used to make art-making more accessible. Engaging in dance, music, or movement-based art can also help improve gross motor skills, balance, and body awareness, particularly for children who struggle with mobility or coordination issues.

Moreover, creative arts can help children with special needs develop emotional regulation and self-awareness. Many children with disabilities experience heightened emotional sensitivities or have difficulty managing their emotions, leading to frustration, anxiety, or behavioral challenges. Art provides a safe space for children to explore their emotions, process difficult feelings, and practice emotional self-regulation. For example, painting or drawing may help a child calm down after a stressful situation, while engaging in rhythmic activities like drumming or dancing can help release pent-up energy and reduce anxiety. In some cases, art therapists work with children to help them use creative arts as a therapeutic tool for managing emotions and building resilience.

Finally, creative arts offer significant benefits for social development. Children with special needs may face challenges in social interaction, particularly those with ASD or social anxiety. Participating in group art projects, theater performances, or music ensembles provides opportunities for collaboration, teamwork, and social communication. In these settings, children learn to share materials, take turns, listen to others' ideas, and work together to achieve a common goal. These experiences promote empathy, cooperation, and a sense of belonging, all of which are essential for building positive relationships with peers.

Adaptive Art Techniques for Cognitive Development

When working with children with special needs, it is essential to adapt artistic activities to meet their specific cognitive, physical, and sensory requirements. Adaptive art techniques involve modifying traditional artistic methods and materials to make them accessible to all learners, regardless of their abilities. These adaptations can range from providing alternative tools and materials to using specific sensory approaches that engage multiple senses and support cognitive development.

For children with cognitive impairments, such as intellectual disabilities or learning disabilities, art activities should be designed to break down complex tasks into smaller, manageable steps. This helps children stay focused and engaged without becoming overwhelmed. For example, rather than expecting a child to complete an entire painting in one session, the activity might be divided into stages, such as choosing colors, outlining shapes, and then filling in sections one at a time. Providing visual cues or step-by-step instructions can also help children understand the process more clearly and feel a sense of accomplishment as they complete each step.

Sensory-based art is particularly beneficial for children with sensory processing disorders or autism. These children may experience either hypersensitivity or hyposensitivity to sensory stimuli, making it difficult for them to engage in traditional classroom activities. Adaptive art techniques that incorporate a variety of textures, temperatures, and tactile sensations can help these children process sensory input more effectively. For example, finger painting with cold, smooth paint, working with textured clay, or using materials like feathers, sandpaper, and fabric can provide sensory-rich experiences that stimulate different parts of the brain and encourage sensory integration.

Children with physical disabilities or mobility challenges may benefit from adaptive tools and modified materials that make the physical act of creating art more accessible. For example, children with limited hand mobility might use large-handled paintbrushes or grip-friendly pencils that are easier to hold and manipulate. Alternatively, children who have difficulty with fine motor control might use touch-sensitive digital art tools, allowing them to create digital paintings or drawings using light touch or adaptive devices. For children in wheelchairs, adjustable art tables or easels that accommodate different heights and angles can make it easier for them to access art supplies and work comfortably.

Collaborative art activities can also be adapted to support cognitive development in children with special needs, particularly those who may struggle with attention, executive function, or social communication. For example, a group mural project might be broken down into smaller tasks, with each child contributing to a specific section of the artwork. This allows children to focus on their individual task while still participating in a larger group project, promoting both cognitive and social development. Additionally, using clear, structured guidelines for group activities can help children with attention-deficit/hyperactivity disorder (ADHD) or executive function challenges stay on track and work collaboratively with their peers.

Music and movement-based art activities provide another avenue for adaptive art techniques, particularly for children with physical or cognitive disabilities. For children who struggle with traditional visual arts, music and dance offer an alternative way to engage with the creative process. Movement-based activities like dance therapy or music improvisation allow children to express themselves through their bodies, helping them develop motor coordination, rhythm, and emotional regulation. These activities are particularly beneficial for children with limited verbal communication skills, as they provide a non-verbal outlet for self-expression and creativity.

Additionally, assistive technology can play a key role in making art accessible to children with special needs. For example, speech-generating devices or digital drawing pads can enable children with communication difficulties to participate in creative arts by using technology to express their ideas visually or verbally. Augmented reality (AR) or virtual reality (VR) tools can also create immersive artistic experiences for children with physical disabilities, allowing them to explore virtual art galleries, create 3D sculptures, or engage in interactive storytelling without physical barriers.

Case Studies of Art-Based Interventions

Art-based interventions have been used in a variety of educational and therapeutic settings to support children with special needs, demonstrating the powerful impact of creative arts on cognitive and emotional development. These interventions often incorporate elements of art therapy, adaptive art techniques, and individualized learning plans to meet the specific needs of each child.

One notable case study is the use of art therapy for children with autism spectrum disorder (ASD) at the Rebecca School in New York City, which serves children with developmental delays and neurodevelopmental disorders. The school incorporates art therapy as a core component of its curriculum, using visual arts, music, and movement to help children with ASD develop their communication skills, sensory processing, and emotional regulation. Art therapists at the Rebecca School work with students individually or in small groups, tailoring art activities to each child's sensory preferences and developmental level. For example, a child who is sensitive to tactile sensations might start by using smooth, dry materials like colored pencils or pastels, gradually introducing more sensory-rich materials like paint or clay as they become more comfortable. Over time, students at the Rebecca School have shown significant improvements in their ability to express their emotions, interact with peers, and engage in creative problem-solving.

Another successful art-based intervention can be seen in the VSA Arts of Georgia program, which focuses on making the arts accessible to individuals with disabilities. One of the program's flagship initiatives involves providing inclusive arts workshops for children with physical and intellectual disabilities, allowing them to explore various art forms such as visual arts, music, and drama. In one case, a child with cerebral palsy participated in an adaptive painting workshop where he used a specially designed head pointer to paint on a canvas. Despite his physical limitations, the child was able to create vibrant, expressive artwork, boosting his confidence and providing him with a sense of accomplishment. This case demonstrates how adaptive art techniques can empower children with physical disabilities to engage in creative expression, building self-esteem and allowing them to experience the joy of artistic creation in ways that may not have been possible with traditional tools or methods.

In a study conducted at The Art Room, a UK-based intervention program that works with children experiencing emotional and behavioral difficulties, art was used as a therapeutic tool to improve emotional well-being and social skills. The program's approach centers on creating a safe, structured environment where children can express themselves through various forms of art, including painting, sculpture, and collage. Many of the children who attend The Art Room have experienced trauma, have mental health challenges, or struggle with social interactions in traditional school settings. By using art as a form of self-expression, these children are able to process difficult emotions, build trust with adults and peers, and gain confidence in their ability to manage their emotions. One case study from The Art Room involved a child who had difficulty controlling their anger and often became disruptive in class. After participating in several art sessions, the child was able to channel their emotions into their artwork, using painting as a way to express frustration and gradually learning to self-regulate their behavior.

Music therapy has also been widely recognized as an effective art-based intervention for children with special needs, particularly those with developmental delays, autism, or speech impairments. In a study conducted by Nordoff-Robbins Music Therapy, children with ASD participated in music therapy sessions designed to encourage communication, social interaction, and emotional expression. The sessions involved activities such as playing instruments, singing, and improvising music, all of which were tailored to the individual needs of each child. One case study from the program highlighted a non-verbal child who began to engage with the therapist by tapping on a drum and humming along to the music. Over time, the child became more vocal, using music as a way to express emotions and communicate with others. The case illustrates how music therapy can help unlock communication potential in children who struggle with verbal language, allowing them to connect with the world around them through sound and rhythm.

Another art-based intervention, Drama Therapy, has been used to support children with ADHD and emotional disturbances. In a case study from The Drama Therapy Institute of Los Angeles, children with ADHD participated in drama-based activities that focused on impulse control, role-playing, and emotional regulation. Through structured dramatic play, the children were encouraged to take on different roles, act out scenarios, and practice self-regulation in a safe and supportive environment. One child, who had difficulty focusing and controlling their impulses, participated in a role-playing game where they had to follow specific instructions and stay in character. The child learned to manage their behavior within the context of the game, practicing attention control and self-discipline in a fun and engaging way. The results of this intervention showed improvements in the child's ability to focus and regulate emotions in both the therapy setting and their daily life.

Visual arts therapy has also been implemented as part of inclusive classrooms, where both neurotypical children and children with special needs engage in art projects together. In a case study from an inclusive art program in Colorado, children with Down syndrome, ADHD, and ASD were paired with neurotypical peers to collaborate on large-scale art installations. These collaborative projects encouraged communication, cooperation, and social interaction among all participants, fostering an inclusive and supportive environment. One notable case involved a child with Down syndrome who had difficulty initiating social interactions. Through the process of working on a mural with peers, the child gradually became more engaged in group discussions, contributing ideas and working alongside others. The child's teachers reported improvements in the child's social confidence and willingness to interact with classmates in other areas of school life as well.

The success of these case studies demonstrates the trans-formative potential of art-based interventions in special needs education. Through the creative arts, children with disabilities are able to access new pathways to learning, communication, and emotional well-being, often achieving breakthroughs that might not be possible through traditional teaching methods alone.

Conclusion

Creative arts hold immense potential for unlocking the cognitive, emotional, and social capabilities of children with special needs. By providing alternative methods of communication, fostering cognitive development, and promoting emotional regulation, the arts offer an inclusive and accessible approach to education that meets the diverse needs of these learners. Adaptive art techniques, ranging from sensory-based activities to technology-enhanced tools, ensure that all children, regardless of ability, can engage in creative expression and experience the joy of artistic creation. The case studies discussed in this chapter highlight the profound impact of art-based interventions in enhancing the lives of children with disabilities, empowering them to reach their full potential. Through continued investment in and exploration of creative arts in special needs education, we can create more inclusive, supportive environments where all children have the opportunity to thrive.

Encouraging Creative Arts at Home

C reating a space for creative arts at home is essential for fostering cognitive growth, emotional well-being, and personal expression in children. While schools play a significant role in nurturing creativity, the home environment can also be a rich ground for artistic exploration, allowing children to express themselves freely and develop important skills. Parents and educators can collaborate to encourage creative activities that not only enhance cognitive development but also promote emotional resilience and social skills. By fostering an artistic environment and providing practical activities, parents can support their children's holistic growth. However, it is equally important to recognize and address the potential barriers that may hinder creative exploration at home.

Fostering an Artistic Environment for Cognitive Growth

An essential part of encouraging creative arts at home is creating a physical and emotional environment that fosters artistic exploration. This involves making space for art supplies, setting aside time for creative activities, and establishing a culture of curiosity and experimentation. By providing an environment that values creativity, parents can help their children develop critical thinking, problem-solving, and emotional regulation skills.

One of the key elements of fostering an artistic environment is providing access to art materials. Having a variety of supplies on hand allows children to experiment with different mediums and discover their creative preferences.

Basic materials such as colored pencils, markers, crayons, paint, clay, and paper are important starting points, but parents can also introduce non-traditional materials like recycled objects, fabric scraps, or natural elements like leaves and twigs. By offering a diverse range of supplies, parents can encourage children to think outside the box and use different textures and colors in their creations, which supports sensory integration and fine motor skills.

Another critical component of fostering creativity is allowing for unstructured time. While structured activities and lessons are valuable, children need time to engage in free play and spontaneous creativity. Unstructured time gives children the freedom to explore their imagination, come up with their own ideas, and make decisions about what to create. This type of play is essential for developing executive function skills, including planning, decision-making, and problem-solving. For example, a child who is given time to create a sculpture from clay without specific instructions will need to think critically about how to shape the material, make adjustments as they go, and decide when the project is complete.

Parents should also consider the emotional environment they are creating at home. Encouraging creativity requires a culture of openness, support, and non-judgment. Children need to feel that their artistic efforts are valued, regardless of the outcome. This means praising the process of creation, not just the final product. A child who feels free to take risks and experiment artistically is more likely to develop cognitive flexibility and resilience. Mistakes and challenges are an inevitable part of the creative process, and teaching children that these moments are opportunities for learning helps them develop a growth mindset, which is critical for cognitive and emotional growth.

In addition to creating a supportive environment for artistic exploration, parents can encourage creativity by modeling artistic behaviors. When parents engage in their own creative activities—whether drawing, painting, cooking, or crafting—they show their children that creativity is a lifelong skill that can be enjoyed at any age. This modeling reinforces the idea that creativity is valuable, and it encourages children to see art as a natural part of everyday life rather than a special activity reserved for school or formal lessons.

Lastly, it is essential to provide opportunities for multi sensory learning within the artistic environment. Children thrive when they can engage multiple senses in their creative activities. For example, parents might encourage children to listen to music while drawing, incorporate tactile elements like sand or fabric into their artwork, or explore the smells and textures of natural materials when creating collages. Multi sensory experiences stimulate different areas of the brain, helping children make connections between their senses and cognitive processes such as memory, attention, and spatial reasoning.

Practical Activities for Parents and Educators

To encourage creative arts at home, parents and educators can engage children in a wide range of activities that stimulate their imagination and cognitive growth. These activities should be designed to challenge children at different developmental stages while allowing them the freedom to explore their ideas in a supportive environment.

1. Drawing and Painting Activities: These classic forms of artistic expression are perfect for developing fine motor skills, hand-eye coordination, and visual-spatial reasoning. Parents can encourage their children to explore a variety of drawing and painting techniques, such as watercolor washes, crayon resist (where children use wax crayons to create a drawing and then paint over it with watercolor), or finger painting for younger children. More advanced drawing exercises, such as observational drawing or portraiture, can help older children develop attention to detail and the ability to see relationships between shapes and proportions.

2. Storytelling and Creative Writing: Storytelling allows children to explore narrative structures, character development, and emotional expression. Parents can introduce creative writing by prompting their children with open-ended questions like, "What would happen if animals could talk?" or "What kind of adventure would you go on if you had magical powers?" For younger children, oral storytelling or creating picture books with illustrations can serve as an introduction to narrative structure. Older children might enjoy writing short stories, poems, or even comic strips, helping them develop language skills, memory, and creative thinking.

3. Sculpture and Building Projects: Working with three-dimensional materials such as clay, play dough, or recycled objects supports spatial awareness and problem-solving skills. Parents can provide materials like modeling clay, cardboard, glue, and found objects for children to create their own sculptures, architectural models, or dioramas. Activities like creating a miniature world (for example, a forest or city made from cardboard and natural materials) encourage imaginative thinking and require children to plan and execute their ideas in a three-dimensional space.

4. Music and Dance: Encouraging children to explore music and movement allows them to express themselves in ways that support cognitive and emotional regulation. Parents can provide instruments such as drums, shakers, or xylophones, or simply encourage children to sing or make their own instruments using household items. Music activities, such as creating rhythms or making up songs, help children develop pattern recognition, memory, and auditory processing skills. Similarly, dance activities encourage body awareness, coordination, and physical expression. Allowing children to create their own dances or improvise to different types of music supports cognitive flexibility and creativity.

5. Collaborative Art Projects: Working on collaborative art projects, such as a family mural or a group sculpture, can help children develop teamwork and communication skills. Collaborative projects teach children how to share

materials, negotiate creative ideas, and work together to achieve a common goal. For example, a parent might lead a group project where each family member contributes to a large painting or sculpture, with the theme and materials being open to creative interpretation. These projects also help children learn about patience and compromise, as they navigate the dynamics of group decision-making.

6. Nature-Inspired Art: Engaging with nature as a source of artistic inspiration fosters environmental awareness and supports cognitive development through sensory exploration. Parents can encourage children to create art using natural materials such as leaves, flowers, stones, and sticks. For example, children might create a nature collage, build a miniature fairy house from twigs and moss, or use leaf rubbings to create patterns and textures. Exploring the natural world through art allows children to develop observational skills and think creatively about how to use materials in new ways.

7. Art-Based Problem-Solving Activities: Parents and educators can challenge children to solve creative problems through art. For example, they might present a problem like, "How can you design a bridge that can hold the weight of a toy car using only cardboard and glue?" or "Can you create a painting using only three colors?" These types of activities encourage innovative thinking and the ability to approach problems from multiple perspectives, fostering both creativity and cognitive resilience.

Overcoming Barriers to Creative Exploration

While fostering an artistic environment at home is highly beneficial, several barriers may hinder creative exploration. Recognizing these obstacles and addressing them effectively is crucial to supporting children's artistic development.

One common barrier is lack of time. In today's fast-paced world, both parents and children often have busy schedules filled with schoolwork, extracurricular activities, and household responsibilities. To overcome this challenge, parents can schedule regular time for creative activities, even if it's just 20 minutes a day. For example, setting aside time for a quick drawing session before dinner or a weekend crafting project can help integrate creativity into the daily routine without overwhelming the schedule.

Another barrier is the fear of mess or disorder. Many parents may feel hesitant to encourage artistic activities at home because of the potential for spills, stains, or clutter. While it's true that creative projects can sometimes be messy, this should not discourage exploration. Parents can designate a specific area in the home—such as a corner of the living room or kitchen table—as an "art zone" where children are free to explore and experiment without fear of making a mess. Using washable materials or placing a tarp or old newspapers under the workspace can also make cleanup easier.

Financial limitations can also pose a challenge for families who may not have access to expensive art supplies or formal art classes. However, fostering creativity doesn't require expensive materials. Parents can encourage children to use everyday objects, recycled materials, or items found in nature to create art. For example, using empty cereal boxes to build sculptures or collecting leaves and twigs for a nature collage are low-cost ways to engage in creative exploration. Additionally, many online resources and tutorials are available for free, offering guidance on art projects and activities that can be done at home with minimal supplies.

A lack of confidence in artistic abilities is another common barrier, both for parents and children. Parents who feel they are not artistically inclined may hesitate to encourage creative activities, fearing they won't be able to guide or support their children effectively. However, it is important to remember that fostering creativity is not about being a professional artist but about encouraging exploration, curiosity, and expression. Parents don't need to have advanced artistic skills to support their children's creativity. In fact, modeling the process of creative discovery—such as trying new things, experimenting with materials, and embracing mistakes—can be a powerful lesson for children. Parents can frame creative activities as a shared experience, where they learn alongside their children, thus fostering a growth mindset in the process.

For children, fear of failure can also be a barrier to creative exploration. Some children may feel discouraged if they think their artwork does not look "good enough" or if they struggle to bring their ideas to life. To overcome this, parents and educators can emphasize the value of the creative process rather than focusing solely on the end product. Celebrating effort, experimentation, and the ability to think outside the box helps children understand that creativity is not about perfection but about innovation and self-expression. Creating an environment where mistakes are viewed as learning opportunities encourages children to take creative risks and build resilience.

Another significant barrier is the overemphasis on structured activities and technology in children's lives. With the proliferation of digital entertainment and structured extracurricular activities, children may have fewer opportunities for unstructured, open-ended creative play. To counter this, parents can make a conscious effort to provide balance by incorporating time for free creative exploration alongside screen time and structured activities. Encouraging children to step away from screens and engage in tactile, sensory experiences—such as drawing, painting, or building with their hands—stimulates different areas of the brain and promotes deeper cognitive engagement.

Lastly, cultural perceptions of the arts can sometimes act as a barrier to creative exploration. In some households, there may be a perception that artistic activities are not as important as academic or athletic achievements. Parents might prioritize homework or sports over creative endeavors, particularly if they view the arts as "frivolous" or lacking practical value. To overcome this, it is essential to shift the narrative around the arts by recognizing their role in fostering critical thinking, problem-solving, and emotional intelligence. Parents can seek out resources, such as research articles or examples of successful individuals who have benefited from a creative background, to gain a deeper understanding of how the arts contribute to cognitive development and long-term success.

Encouraging Creative Arts for All Ages

Creative exploration should not be limited to young children. While early childhood is a critical period for developing cognitive and motor skills through the arts, older children and adolescents also benefit significantly from creative activities. Parents can continue to support artistic expression as their children grow, offering age-appropriate challenges that cater to their evolving interests and abilities.

For young children, focusing on sensory-rich experiences that engage their fine motor skills, spatial awareness, and creativity is essential. As children grow older, they may become more interested in exploring different techniques, developing skills in specific artistic disciplines, and engaging in more complex projects. For example, an older child might take on projects that involve learning new mediums, such as acrylic painting or digital art, while adolescents might enjoy experimenting with creative writing, photography, or music composition. By offering age-appropriate tools and activities, parents can keep the spark of creativity alive through all developmental stages.

In adolescence, creativity becomes a critical tool for self-expression and identity exploration. At this stage, teens often use art, music, writing, or performance as a means to explore their emotions, process life experiences, and develop their sense of self. Parents can encourage this exploration by supporting their teens' interests in specific artistic endeavors and giving them the freedom to express themselves authentically. For example, an adolescent who enjoys photography might be encouraged to document their surroundings and experiment with different styles, while a teen interested in music might benefit from composing their own songs or experimenting with digital music production.

Creative arts also help adolescents build emotional resilience, as they learn to channel their feelings and thoughts into productive outlets. This emotional outlet is especially important for managing the stress, anxiety, and pressures that often accompany adolescence. Parents can provide the space, resources, and encouragement for their teenagers to engage in creative projects, whether that involves writing, painting, music, or even drama. Allowing adolescents to take ownership of their creative process fosters independence, confidence, and emotional intelligence, all of which are critical for personal and academic success.

Moreover, creative activities that require collaboration—such as group art projects, theater performances, or music ensembles—help teens develop social skills and teamwork. Engaging in these activities teaches adolescents how to communicate, share ideas, and work together toward a common goal, which can improve their ability to collaborate with others in school, work, and future relationships. Encouraging teens to join local art clubs, community theater groups, or music bands can provide them with social outlets that also nurture their creativity.

For both children and teens, creative arts at home can serve as a powerful complement to the structured learning they receive in school. By fostering a home environment that values artistic exploration, parents help their children develop cognitive flexibility, critical thinking skills, and emotional resilience. These skills are essential not only for academic achievement but also for personal growth, helping children and adolescents navigate the complexities of life with confidence and creativity.

In conclusion, fostering creative arts at home offers parents a unique opportunity to support their children's holistic development. By creating an environment that encourages artistic exploration, providing access to practical activities, and addressing barriers to creativity, parents can help their children develop essential cognitive, emotional, and social skills. Creative arts are more than just a pastime; they are a foundation for lifelong learning, self-expression, and problem-solving. Parents who invest in nurturing creativity at home provide their children with the tools they need to succeed in all areas of life.

The Future of Creative Arts in Education

T he future of creative arts in education is poised to undergo significant transformations as emerging trends and advancements in technology reshape how students engage with artistic practices. Creative arts have long been recognized for their profound influence on cognitive growth, emotional development, and social skills. However, as educational paradigms evolve in response to the digital age, creative arts are also adapting to integrate technology, new methodologies, and innovative teaching approaches that promise to deepen their impact on learning. This chapter explores the emerging trends in art-based learning, examines the intersection of technology and creative arts, and discusses the lasting influence of the arts on lifelong learning.

Emerging Trends in Art-Based Learning

The integration of creative arts into mainstream education continues to expand, driven by a growing recognition of the arts' role in promoting cognitive flexibility, problem-solving, and emotional intelligence. Several key trends are reshaping how creative arts are delivered in schools and other learning environments, making art-based learning more accessible, interdisciplinary, and impact.

One of the most significant trends is the increased emphasis on interdisciplinary learning, where creative arts are integrated with STEM (Science, Technology, Engineering, and Math) subjects to form what is now widely known as STEAM (Science, Technology, Engineering, Arts, and Math). STEAM education recognizes the importance of creativity in scientific inquiry and problem-solving, positioning the arts as an essential component of holistic learning. In a STEAM-based curriculum, students might engage in activities that blend artistic expression with engineering concepts, such as designing prototypes through digital 3D modeling software or exploring the intersection of physics and visual art by creating light installations that demonstrate principles of reflection and refraction. By incorporating the arts into STEM fields, educators are encouraging students to think creatively about scientific and technical challenges, promoting both critical thinking and innovation.

Another trend shaping the future of art-based learning is the rise of personalized and adaptive learning platforms that allow students to engage in creative arts at their own pace and according to their unique learning styles. Digital tools and platforms enable educators to design customized art-based learning experiences that cater to individual student needs, making art education more inclusive. For example, students who are more inclined toward music composition might have access to digital audio workstations that let them experiment with sound, rhythm, and melody in real time. Meanwhile, students interested in visual arts might use digital drawing tablets and software to explore different artistic techniques and styles. Personalized learning platforms also provide opportunities for formative assessment, where teachers can track student progress and offer tailored feedback to support growth in specific areas of creativity.

Furthermore, there is a growing emphasis on project-based learning (PBL) in the arts, which allows students to work on real-world, long-term projects that integrate multiple subjects and artistic disciplines. PBL encourages students to take ownership of their learning by engaging in meaningful, hands-on experiences that require critical thinking, collaboration, and creativity. For example, in an art-based PBL activity, students might be tasked with designing a public art installation for their community, incorporating elements of architecture, environmental science, and cultural history into their project. By working on these complex, interdisciplinary projects, students develop practical skills that prepare them for future academic and career challenges, while also deepening their understanding of how the arts intersect with other fields.

Mindfulness and social-emotional learning (SEL) are also becoming integral components of art-based education. Creative arts have long been associated with promoting emotional expression and self-regulation, and this trend is gaining traction as schools prioritize SEL to help students navigate stress, build resilience, and foster empathy. Art therapy techniques, such as visual journalism, mandala creation, and movement-based practices like dance and yoga, are increasingly being integrated into classrooms to support students' mental health and emotional well-being. These practices allow students to develop a greater awareness of their emotions and provide healthy outlets for self-expression. Incorporating mindfulness into art education helps students manage their emotional responses and improves their ability to focus and engage with their work.

Lastly, globalization and cultural exchange are playing an important role in shaping the future of creative arts education. As the world becomes more interconnected, art-based learning is expanding to incorporate diverse cultural perspectives, artistic traditions, and global themes. This trend emphasizes the importance of teaching students to appreciate the diversity of artistic expression and to use art as a means of cross-cultural communication. Programs that promote global collaboration—such as virtual art exchanges, where students from different countries work together on shared creative projects—offer opportunities for learners to engage with different cultural aesthetics and narratives. These experiences help students develop a broader understanding of global issues while fostering a sense of global citizenship.

Technology, Art, and Cognitive Growth

The integration of technology into the creative arts is one of the most transformative forces shaping the future of art education. Advancements in digital tools, artificial intelligence, and virtual reality (VR) are opening up new possibilities for artistic expression and cognitive development. As technology becomes more deeply embedded in the creative process, it is reshaping how students engage with the arts, offering opportunities for more immersive, interactive, and personalized learning experiences.

One of the most significant technological innovations in art education is the rise of digital art tools and platforms. Digital drawing tablets, 3D modeling software, and virtual design platforms are becoming increasingly common in classrooms, providing students with new ways to explore visual arts. These tools offer unique advantages over traditional media, as they allow students to experiment with a wide range of techniques, textures, and colors without the limitations of physical materials. For example, students can use digital tools to create intricate illustrations, animate characters, or design virtual environments that would be difficult to achieve with conventional methods. This type of digital experimentation fosters cognitive flexibility by encouraging students to think critically about how to apply different artistic techniques to achieve specific outcomes.

Virtual reality (VR) and augmented reality (AR) are also making their way into creative arts education, offering students immersive experiences that engage multiple senses and enhance cognitive growth. VR allows students to step inside virtual galleries, explore famous works of art in 3D, or even create their own virtual sculptures and installations. This level of immersion can deepen students' understanding of artistic concepts by allowing them to interact with art in a more tactile and experiential way. For example, a student studying Renaissance architecture might use VR to virtually explore the intricate details of a historical cathedral, gaining a more comprehensive understanding of its design and structure than they could from textbooks alone. These immersive experiences stimulate spatial reasoning, visual memory, and problem-solving skills by requiring students to navigate complex virtual environments and make creative decisions in real time.

Artificial intelligence (AI) and machine learning are also being applied to art education, enabling students to engage with technology in new and innovative ways. AI tools can assist students in generating creative ideas, offering suggestions for improving compositions, or even helping them analyze the structure of their artwork. For instance, AI-powered applications might suggest color palettes or recommend adjustments to the composition of a digital painting, giving students real-time feedback on their work. In addition to offering practical guidance, AI-driven tools can also foster cognitive growth by encouraging students to experiment with different styles and techniques that they may not have considered on their own. This type of AI-enhanced learning encourages exploratory thinking and creative problem-solving by challenging students to push the boundaries of their artistic practice.

Interactive art installations and digital media are also gaining prominence in creative arts education. These installations often combine technology, visual arts, sound, and motion to create immersive environments that engage students' senses and emotions. By interacting with digital installations, students can explore the relationship between technology and art, learning how to use code, sensors, and other technological tools to create dynamic, responsive artworks. This intersection of technology and art fosters computational thinking and systems thinking, as students must understand how various components work together to create an interactive experience. Furthermore, these installations encourage collaboration, as students often work in teams to build and troubleshoot complex digital projects.

Gamification is another trend that is transforming art-based learning through technology. By incorporating game-like elements into artistic activities—such as challenges, rewards, and interactive storytelling—educators can increase student engagement and motivation. For example, a gamified art project might involve students creating characters, environments, or narratives that are integrated into a digital game or interactive story. This approach not only makes art more accessible and enjoyable but also promotes critical thinking and problem-solving by requiring students to consider the rules, logic, and structure of the game as they develop their artwork.

While technology offers many advantages for creative arts education, it also raises important questions about the balance between digital and traditional media. Educators must ensure that the introduction of technology does not diminish the value of hands-on, tactile art-making experiences, which are crucial for developing fine motor skills and sensory awareness. Instead, technology should be viewed as a complementary tool that enhances, rather than replaces, traditional artistic practices.

The Lasting Impact of Creative Arts on Lifelong Learning

The benefits of creative arts education extend far beyond the classroom, shaping students' cognitive, emotional, and social development in ways that contribute to lifelong learning. By fostering creativity, critical thinking, and problem-solving skills, the arts equip individuals with the tools they need to adapt and thrive in an ever-changing world.

One of the most significant long-term impacts of creative arts education is the development of cognitive flexibility and adaptive thinking. Engaging in artistic activities requires students to think creatively, explore multiple perspectives, and experiment with different approaches to problem-solving. These skills are essential for navigating complex, real-world challenges, where solutions are often not straightforward or predetermined. For example, individuals who have developed strong creative problem-solving abilities through their arts education are more likely to approach challenges with an open mind, think critically about possible solutions, and adapt their strategies as needed. This cognitive flexibility is especially valuable in today's workforce, where innovation and adaptability are increasingly important.

Creative arts education also plays a critical role in promoting emotional intelligence and empathy, both of which are essential for building meaningful relationships and navigating social dynamics throughout life. Artistic activities, whether in visual arts, music, theater, or dance, allow individuals to explore their own emotions and the emotions of others, fostering deeper understanding and emotional awareness. For example, engaging in drama or role-playing exercises encourages individuals to step into different characters' shoes, gaining insight into their thoughts, feelings, and motivations. This practice of perspective-taking enhances empathy, which is crucial for developing strong interpersonal relationships, resolving conflicts, and working effectively in teams. As individuals carry these skills into adulthood, they are better equipped to navigate personal and professional relationships with emotional intelligence, compassion, and understanding.

Moreover, the self-expression fostered by creative arts education has lasting implications for personal well-being and mental health. Throughout life, individuals encounter various emotional and psychological challenges, and the ability to express feelings through creative outlets can serve as an important coping mechanism. Whether through journalism, painting, playing music, or performing, the arts offer an outlet for processing complex emotions, relieving stress, and gaining insight into one's inner world. This form of self-expression is linked to improved emotional regulation, which helps individuals manage stress and maintain mental well-being in the face of life's challenges. People who develop strong artistic habits early in life are more likely to continue using creative expression as a tool for self-care and emotional resilience in adulthood.

Creative arts also promote lifelong curiosity and a love for learning, as they encourage individuals to approach the world with wonder, creativity, and an open mind. Artistic exploration often leads to questions about different cultures, historical contexts, or scientific principles, sparking curiosity and a desire to learn more. For instance, a student who creates a painting inspired by a historical event might become interested in learning more about that period, while a student who designs a sculpture based on natural forms might be inspired to explore biology or environmental science. This interdisciplinary curiosity fosters a growth mindset, where individuals view learning as an ongoing, dynamic process rather than a finite pursuit. The ability to approach new ideas and experiences with curiosity and creativity is a critical skill for adapting to the changing demands of the modern world, where continuous learning is essential for both personal and professional development.

In addition to personal benefits, creative arts education has a profound impact on professional success across a wide range of fields. The cognitive skills developed through artistic practices—such as problem-solving, critical thinking, and innovation—are highly valued in the modern workforce. Employers increasingly seek individuals who can think creatively, collaborate effectively, and approach challenges with innovative solutions. For example, professionals in fields like technology, business, and healthcare benefit from the ability to approach problems from multiple perspectives and generate original ideas. Creative thinking is also essential for entrepreneurship and leadership, as it enables individuals to develop new products, services, or strategies that address emerging needs or market opportunities. By fostering creativity and cognitive flexibility, arts education prepares individuals for success in a rapidly evolving economy that demands adaptability, innovation, and resilience.

The impact of creative arts on community engagement and social change is another significant aspect of lifelong learning. Artistic expression has long been a powerful tool for social commentary, activism, and cultural preservation. Individuals who have developed a deep understanding of the arts are often more engaged in civic and community life, using their creative talents to address social issues, raise awareness, or promote positive change. Whether through public art installations, socially conscious performances, or community-based art projects, individuals with a strong foundation in the arts are better positioned to contribute to the cultural and social fabric of their communities. This sense of civic responsibility and community engagement is a lasting legacy of arts education, as it empowers individuals to use their creativity to inspire change and foster a more inclusive, compassionate society.

Furthermore, the creative arts play a vital role in the development of cultural literacy and global awareness. Exposure to diverse artistic traditions, whether through visual art, music, literature, or performance, helps individuals appreciate the richness and diversity of human expression. Understanding different cultures through their artistic output fosters greater empathy, tolerance, and respect for diversity, which are essential qualities in an increasingly interconnected and globalized world. As individuals engage with various cultural forms throughout their lives, they build the capacity to bridge cultural divides, appreciate different perspectives, and contribute to cross-cultural dialogue and collaboration. This global awareness is critical not only for fostering harmony in multicultural societies but also for addressing global challenges that require cooperation and understanding across borders.

Finally, the lasting impact of creative arts on lifelong learning is evident in the role of arts-based learning for older adults. As individuals age, engaging in creative activities remains a powerful tool for maintaining cognitive health, enhancing memory, and promoting emotional well-being. Studies have shown that participation in creative arts—whether through painting, music, dance, or writing—can help older adults preserve cognitive function, improve social engagement, and reduce feelings of isolation. For example, older adults who participate in music-making or visual arts programs often report improved mood, greater social connection, and enhanced cognitive sharpness. These benefits highlight the value of creative arts not only for young learners but also for individuals across the lifespan, underscoring the importance of nurturing creativity as a lifelong endeavor.

In conclusion, the future of creative arts in education is marked by exciting developments in technology, interdisciplinary learning, and personalized approaches to artistic exploration. As emerging trends continue to reshape the way students engage with the arts, the impact of creative arts education on cognitive growth, emotional intelligence, and lifelong learning remains profound. By fostering creativity, critical thinking, and self-expression, the arts equip individuals with the skills they need to thrive in a dynamic and ever-changing world. From early childhood to adulthood, the creative arts serve as a cornerstone for intellectual and emotional development, promoting resilience, curiosity, and a deep appreciation for the richness of human experience. As we look to the future, it is clear that creative arts will continue to play a pivotal role in shaping the minds and hearts of learners for generations to come.

Conclusion

U nleashing the full potential of cognitive growth through creativity is not only a goal for educators and parents but a societal responsibility that extends to policymakers and communities. Creative arts have long been valued for their ability to foster imagination, self-expression, and emotional intelligence, but their deeper impact on cognitive development and lifelong learning is becoming increasingly clear. In a world that demands adaptability, critical thinking, and innovation, the role of creative arts in shaping the cognitive capabilities of individuals from early childhood through adulthood is more essential than ever. For parents, educators, and policymakers, understanding the trans-formative power of creative arts and making concerted efforts to integrate them into educational systems and home environments is key to unlocking human potential.

Key Takeaways for Parents, Educators, and Policy Makers

The critical role of creative arts in cognitive development cannot be over-stated. From the earliest stages of development, artistic activities stimulate brain function, helping children build neural connections that support higher-order thinking, memory, problem-solving, and emotional regulation. The arts allow children to explore multiple ways of thinking, break away from linear processes, and engage in creative risk-taking, all of which are essential for cognitive flexibility and lifelong learning. As such, parents, educators, and policymakers must prioritize creative arts as an essential component of learning, equal in importance to more traditional academic subjects.

For parents, the key takeaway is the importance of fostering an environment at home that encourages artistic exploration. Parents do not need to be artists themselves to provide their children with the tools and support needed to engage in creative activities. Simple, everyday art supplies like pencils, paint, clay, or musical instruments can become the foundation for rich cognitive development. Parents should value the process of creativity rather than focusing on the final product, encouraging their children to experiment, take risks, and learn from their artistic endeavors. Parents also need to set aside regular time for unstructured, imaginative play, as this kind of play is vital for developing cognitive skills such as executive function, planning, and critical thinking. Engaging in family-based creative activities can also model positive artistic behaviors and demonstrate that creativity is a lifelong pursuit.

For educators, the takeaway is to continue incorporating creative arts into the curriculum in meaningful ways, understanding that arts education is not simply a "supplemental" part of learning but a critical driver of cognitive growth. Educators should integrate the arts across disciplines, allowing students to see the connections between subjects like math, science, literature, and the visual or performing arts. By using project-based learning (PL) and interdisciplinary approaches like STEAM, educators can show students how creative thinking enhances problem-solving and critical analysis in various contexts. Teachers should also embrace adaptive art techniques that cater to diverse learners, including students with special needs, ensuring that creative arts remain accessible and inclusive. Art-based learning should be flexible, open-ended, and student-driven, fostering a sense of ownership and encouraging independent, critical thinking.

For policymakers, the key takeaway is to recognize and support the role of creative arts in education through sustained funding, curriculum development, and research initiatives. Policymakers must ensure that schools are equipped with the necessary resources—such as art supplies, digital tools, and professional development opportunities for teachers—to make arts education accessible and effective for all students. Policies should also encourage partnerships between schools and local arts organizations, allowing students to benefit from exposure to professional artists and cultural institutions. Furthermore, arts education must be integrated into broader educational reforms, particularly as educational systems shift toward interdisciplinary learning and 21st-century skills. Policymakers should work to ensure that creative arts are not sidelined by standardized testing or curriculum requirements but are given equal priority as an integral part of cognitive development.

The Lasting Importance of Creative Arts in Cognitive Development

The lasting impact of creative arts on cognitive development extends far beyond the classroom. Engaging in artistic practices from an early age builds a foundation for skills that are critical for success in today's world: innovation, adaptability, collaboration, and emotional intelligence. These skills are not only relevant for academic achievement but also for professional success, personal fulfillment, and social well-being.

One of the most important long-term cognitive benefits of engaging with creative arts is the development of problem-solving skills. The creative process, whether through visual arts, music, dance, or drama, requires individuals to engage in complex problem-solving tasks, such as figuring out how to convey an idea, balance composition, or structure a performance. In doing so, individuals develop cognitive flexibility, the ability to think critically, and the capacity to approach challenges from multiple perspectives. This type of thinking is not confined to the arts but is transferable to all areas of life, whether in academic pursuits, careers, or personal challenges.

Emotional intelligence is another lasting benefit of creative arts. By providing a safe space for emotional exploration and expression, the arts help individuals develop a deeper understanding of their own emotions and the emotions of others. This emotional literacy is key to building healthy relationships, resolving conflicts, and maintaining mental well-being. Throughout life, the ability to process and express emotions in constructive ways can help individuals navigate difficult situations and maintain resilience in the face of adversity. Moreover, the empathy fostered through engagement with the arts—particularly through collaborative and performance-based activities— enables individuals to connect with others on a deeper level, building stronger communities and promoting social harmony.

The arts also play a crucial role in fostering lifelong learning. By encouraging curiosity, exploration, and creativity, the arts instill a love for learning that transcends formal education. Individuals who have been exposed to creative arts early in life are more likely to continue seeking out new experiences, knowledge, and opportunities for growth. Whether through attending cultural events, pursuing hobbies, or engaging in creative practices, the arts contribute to a mindset of continual growth and discovery. This approach to learning is critical in an era where adaptability and continuous skill development are increasingly necessary for success in the workforce and beyond.

Furthermore, the arts foster a sense of agency and empowerment in individuals. The ability to create something from one's imagination and bring it to life builds confidence and a sense of accomplishment. This feeling of empowerment extends to other areas of life, as individuals who feel confident in their creative abilities are more likely to take risks, pursue their goals, and embrace challenges. The creative arts teach individuals that failure is a natural part of the learning process and that perseverance leads to growth. This resilience, combined with the ability to adapt and innovate, equips individuals with the skills needed to navigate an increasingly complex and uncertain world.

In addition to cognitive and emotional benefits, the creative arts contribute to social and cultural awareness. Through exposure to diverse artistic traditions, individuals gain a deeper understanding of different cultures, histories, and perspectives. This cultural literacy fosters empathy, tolerance, and a greater appreciation for diversity. In an interconnected global society, the ability to understand and appreciate cultural differences is essential for building inclusive communities and addressing global challenges. The arts provide a powerful platform for cross-cultural dialogue and collaboration, enabling individuals to connect with others across boundaries of language, nationality, and identity.

Finally, the creative arts offer enduring benefits for mental health and well-being. Engaging in artistic practices has been shown to reduce stress, improve mood, and promote a sense of fulfillment. Whether through creating visual art, playing music, dancing, or writing, individuals can use the arts as a means of self-care and emotional release. In a world where mental health challenges are on the rise, the creative arts provide a valuable tool for maintaining balance and well-being. Individuals who engage with the arts throughout their lives are better equipped to cope with the stresses of daily life and find meaning and purpose in their experiences.

In conclusion, the full potential of cognitive growth through creativity can only be realized when creative arts are fully integrated into educational systems, home environments, and societal values. For parents, educators, and policymakers, this means prioritizing creative arts as a core component of learning, recognizing their profound impact on cognitive development, emotional intelligence, and lifelong learning. The arts are not an "extra" but an essential part of human development, equipping individuals with the skills, mindset, and resilience needed to thrive in a complex and ever-changing world. As we look to the future, the importance of creative arts in unleashing human potential will only continue to grow, shaping individuals who are not only academically successful but also creative, empathetic, and adaptable lifelong learners.

www.ingramcontent.com/pod-product-compliance
Lightning Source LLC
Chambersburg PA
CBHW071511220526
45472CB00003B/980